362·7

WORKING WITH GIRLS AND YOUNG WOMEN
IN
COMMUNITY SETTINGS

For Ann Rose

Working with Girls and Young Women in Community Settings

Janet Batsleer

Published by
Arena
Ashgate Publishing Limited
Gower House
Croft Road
Aldershot
Hants GU11 3HR
England

Ashgate Publishing Company
Old Post Road
Brookfield
Vermont 05036
USA

British Library Cataloguing in Publication Data

Batsleer, Janet
Working with girls and young women in
community settings
1. Social work with teenagers   2. Social work
with women
I. Title
362.7'083

Library of Congress Catalog Card Number: 96-85510

ISBN 1 85742 303 8

Phototypeset in Palatino by Raven Typesetters, Chester
Printed in Great Britain at University Press, Cambridge

Contents

Acknowledgements

This book exists because there has been a movement within youth and community work practice which was referred to as 'the girls' work movement'. It is an attempt to record some of the work that has gone on. More immediately, it exists because of the encouragement of particular colleagues and the sense that 'something should be written down'. I hope much more will be written down, and not only by women employed in academic departments.

I have had real support and encouragement from friends and colleagues in the Department of Applied Community Studies, and from students and staff in the Women's Studies MA course team at Manchester Metropolitan University. Specific help in the form of supply of documents and references, discussions about particular ideas, reading of early drafts, encouragement to press on, and support in domestic and family life has come from many people. I have tried to keep a note of all the people who have helped in these ways, and I record their names here:

Gregory Batsleer
Julian Batsleer
Margaret Beetham
Erica Burman
Sue Campbell
Sylvia Caveney
Kate Clements
Sue Cockerell
Jill Dennis
Sakinna Dickinson
Maureen Green
Steph Green
Lorraine Hansford
Moira Hill

Netta Hughes
Kath Hunter
Rehana Hussein
Julia Keenan
Kate Kirk
Ken Leech
Mary Madden
Lydia Merrill
Debbie Mitchell
Louise Murray
Liz Neat
Cath Nicholls
Carol Packham
Bhaggi Patel

Nikki Patterson	Yasmin Sonne
Poddy Peerman	Michelle Walmsley
Janet Preece	Viv Whitaker
Mark Smith	Vanessa Worrell
Pavinder Sohal	Margaret White
Alima Sonne	Tracy Yankowski

I would like to thank all the projects from whose reports and publications I have drawn in compiling this book. Where I have drawn on project reports, on group discussions with workers or on the work of youth and community work students, this is acknowledged in the text.

None of the people I have named is to be taken to task for the argument this book tries to develop, or its limitations. I hope they will continue to discuss and debate with me, pointing out the limitations of this book, and contributing, both by writing and by the practice of community-based informal education, to a body of knowledge to which this book is a small contribution.

Janet Batsleer
June 1996

1 Introduction

'Threat'

Somehow, youth work and informal education that focuses attention on girls has always been associated with threat. It seems to be a threat to the boys, who have been getting more than their fair share of attention. It seems to be a threat to long-held assumptions about who and what youth work and informal education are for, and to the 'we've always done it this way' school of practice. And it is initially threatening to women, as well as energising, to realise that 'the way things are' is not as inevitable as the weather, but can change.

Yet this practice which seems so threatening is itself always under threat. First, it was under threat from the boys: banging on the door and demanding to be let in to the girls' night. Then the persuasions of supportive professionals were also potentially threatening: 'There is such a need for progressive and supportive work with boys.' Of course, this is true. Yet there is still a threat to anti-sexist work with girls from anti-sexist work with boys – a threat to budgets, and a threat to the agenda-setting power of autonomous work with girls. In the fashionable world of youth and community work, girls' work was out before it had had the chance to come in.

Attention is turned to 'anti-discriminatory practice'. Of course, recognising the impact of patterns of discrimination on the lives of young people and communities is essential to any good practice in informal education. Sometimes, the concept of 'anti-discriminatory practice' can be used to build on autonomous work with girls, deepening and extending it. Just as often, it can mean that the foundations of the work are forgotten and shaken in the bland machinery of policy-making, where discrimination is opposed in principle and in general, and less and less can be done in practice and specifically.

Now the threat to anti-sexist work with girls and young women is crude once more, and much more powerful than the threat from the boys who were

1

banging on the door: closure; cutbacks; the numbers game; measurable outcomes. Since 1986, when the National Association of Youth Clubs (NAYC) closed down its Girls' Work Unit, which had provided a national focus for the work from the early 1980s, the backlash against positive and progressive work with girls has gathered strength. The resistance to the closure of that unit was strong and swift, and clearly surprised the NAYC. Youth Clubs UK (the new name for the NAYC) is now the organiser of one of the national events which provides an annual focus for the work.

In the 1990s, as Kerry Young has observed, youth work with girls has seemed both well established and curiously vulnerable:

> As the years have passed it has become increasingly easy to organise activities days and concentrate our emphasis on establishing groups for girls. To a certain extent that aspect of our work has gained some acceptability – credibility even. But the purpose of the work, like the purpose of so many other youth and community work methods, has become blurred at the edges. If the general gist of contemporary literature on the subject (little that there is) is anything to go by, it may even be that the purpose of working with girls and young women has become obscured at its very centre. The purpose of the work was never so narrow as simply providing space and opportunity for young women on their own. Specific work with young women, whilst important in its own right, was also (and remains) the central plank by which the challenge to sexism in youth and community work was and is still to be forged. (Young, 1992, p.17)

Has the threat of anti-sexist work with girls and young women become blurred, while the threat to the work is absolutely apparent?

As with so many other aspects of the women's movement, this is a period of transformation. This book is not a swansong, although when I began to write it, I feared that it might be. It is in part a testimony, because we must leave evidence or too much work is lost. I hope that it contains some inspirations. In the main, it is meant to be a guidebook to aspects of work in a 1990s context.

Stories about practice as a source of knowledge

I can make no claims to having undertaken a systematic survey of practice. I am drawing primarily on knowledge I have gained as a tutor in youth and community work studies over the past seven years. As a tutor, I am always on the receiving end of stories about the work. I have come to value these stories and the discussion about them as much as any theoretical framework that we have devised. I also receive project reports, invitations to conferences and meetings, and have access to the library. These are the sources on which what I hope is a systematic reflection presented in this book has drawn.

In this book, I am attempting to offer a context for some of the stories I have heard, to trace the connections between them and between the stories of youth and community work practice and other aspects of contemporary communities and society. Because, as a tutor, I have mainly been concerned with supporting and assessing workers – both part-time and full-time – I have a particular interest in and concern for the strength and well-being of women workers. My colleague, Ann Rose, first introduced me to the term 'conscious use of self in relation to others'. This phrase in many ways encapsulates the concerns of this book. Informal education draws heavily on relationships and therefore on the self. Self-understanding, and the ability to draw on that self-understanding to assist others, has long been recognised as a central professional task, and for women, this can be a highly subversive activity. Patterns of mutual support, including reflection and analysis, are essential to women if we are to continue to build up our strength. I hope that this book will contribute something to this process. The major focus of the book is therefore on questions facing workers in practice.

Feminist practice

The book advocates a feminist practice and also recognises the need to expand and change the meaning of the term 'feminism' so as to embrace the struggles for emancipation and justice of all women, and not simply to make a claim for equality with men of the same class or caste (hooks, 1984). Feminism is understood as the theoretical and political perspective which aims to end sexist patterns of oppression, and which makes coalition and common cause with other perspectives which resist domination and oppression. The feminist practice which this book embraces is therefore necessarily pluralist and diverse. It does not envisage either a single source of women's oppression or a single ending to it.

In recent years, much attention has been given by feminist writers (and writers who do not call themselves feminists but are concerned with the 'gender question') to the question of commonality and difference. In the first instance, this applied to the question of commonalities and differences between men and women. It is linked to a political debate about the appropriateness of demands for equal rights with men, at the same time as recognising and valuing women's 'sexual difference'. Secondly, attention to the question of 'commonality and difference' arises from the recognition that finding yourself belonging to the category 'woman' does not necessarily mean finding yourself to be a member of a group which shares the same social experience, let alone the same biology. People who are positioned within the category 'woman' are enormously different. And some of the differences between women are also marks of powerful divisions and injustices: poverty and comfort (even wealth), and patterns of racism based on nationality, language or skin colour are very obvious examples. They are not merely differences, but become highly significant differences. It is specifically to these significant differences that a feminism with a strong commitment to justice is drawn.

Feminist practice and the politics of difference

For some writers and activists, the whole question of difference and division between women has become so problematic that they no longer see separate and autonomous work with women as an appropriate focus for activism and organisation. Against this perspective, I argue for a recognition of the continuing strength of the category 'woman' as a means for positioning and subordinating us. In the binary opposition man/woman, woman occupies the subordinate position. To organise within the category 'woman' is to organise against subordination. It is a necessary place from which to resist. The recognition of difference then becomes a resource for resisting and challenging oppression which depends in part on a construction of 'woman' as uniform and the same, and defined by a uniform experience of biology.

Iris Young has drawn on the thinking of Jean-Paul Sartre to argue that it is possible to conceptualise women as sharing membership of a series which exists passively in relation to enforced heterosexuality and in relation to a sexual division of labour in which those who care for babies and bodies are defined in distinction to those who do not. Being positioned in such a way does not imply shared experience, shared identity or shared interpretations, but women can choose to become a group in relation to that positionality. It is this active self-naming and grouping which enables feminist practice to occur. Such feminist practice, at its best, in turn challenges the sense that all women are 'the same', and values difference as a resource in the movement for emancipation (Young, 1994).

This understanding of the positionality of 'woman' also allows us to understand some key social elements in the transition from girlhood to womanhood. From the point of view of feminist practice in informal education, growing up as a woman is a social process which changes from generation to generation and yet has some key boundaries. The 'marks of womanhood' are defined in subordination to the marks of male adulthood, in particular in women's relation to heterosexuality and in the responsibility to care for bodies and babies. Feminist practice works from a recognition of these positionings as they structure the lives of young women and also seeks to explore and identify the different relationships which different young women have to the process of 'becoming a woman'. For it is in these real, historical differences that the friction and creativity of change is to be found. And it is the friction and creativity of change which is constantly challenging the positioning of women as subordinate.

When 'difference' is addressed, it is also possible to reveal areas of privilege and the ways difference can be mobilised to reinforce privilege. Significant differences are not just a sign of diversity. I have tried to give an account of the practice of informal, community-based education with girls and young women which recognises and acknowledges diversity and sees it as a strength. It is also important to see how significant differences are 'power-charged'. The problem of the agenda of women's movements being dominated by the voices of already relatively privileged women can then more easily be addressed.

The question of the role of the woman worker inevitably also touches on questions of inequality and injustice among women, of differential access to power and resources. The project of coalition-building is an essential strategy advocated in this book. One of the critical problems for coalition-building is the question of 'on whose terms' coalitions can be built. An analysis of the power relations between women is an essential aspect of coalition-building.

Chapter outline

The early chapters of the book – on the history of the work with girls, the principles of practice and the role of the woman worker – attempt to offer a broad picture of the current situation. They show the diversity among women who carry out youth work: Black women and White women from different classes and communities, lesbians, bisexual women, heterosexual women. I hope that the stories the book tells do reflect some of the diversity of youth and community work practice. Later chapters focus on key social themes that have arisen in relation to practice, and key problems which workers face when delivering programmes of social and political education: sexuality, health and poverty, violence, disability, culture and community are the themes I have chosen. Finally, the book returns to the context of the work and offers some thoughts about new coalitions towards the year 2000.

2 Girls in the modern world: Moments of danger and delight

The 1880s: The girls' clubs

Maude Stanley's volume, *Clubs for Working Girls*, published in 1890, contains a mixture of handy hints and ideological resonance which the present volume can scarcely hope to emulate. She writes for ladies who are interested in the rapid spread of girls' clubs – 'this most modern of schemes':

> it is from the repeated requests of ladies who wish to form new ones, who consult us as to how they should begin, what rules they should have, how often they should get together the girls that these pages are written, in the hope that they may assist others in the work of which we have such pleasing experiences. (Stanley, 1890, p.14)

However lady-like her approach, Maude Stanley – founder of the Soho Club and recorder of the work of the Girls' Club Union – clearly knew her business. Anyone who has tried, in the face of lack of support and understanding, to establish provision for girls in a youth club will recognise her account of disruption and near anarchy. One hundred years later, we can still hear the boys banging at the windows and barging through the doors:

> We remember one sad night when two bigger girls who were sitting happily at work round a little table with a bright lamp, while a story was read to them, suddenly quarrelled about a thimble, and in a passion one girl threw the table over, the others, mad with excitement, began to act in the wildest, utterly indescribable fashion. The unfortunate teacher seized the dangerous lamp, which went out in her hands and came downstairs to get help. Meanwhile the girls threw up the window, and hanging out of it, with loud shouts and rude laughter presently had a crowd underneath, with whom they exchanged chaff and abuse. Downstairs the crowded kitchen was too noisy in its play for any upstairs sounds to be audible.

They, however, were cautioned to be quiet while the ladies went upstairs with a lamp to quell the disturbance and close the window. Coming down with the subdued and sulky girls, found hiding in corners and tolerably ashamed of themselves, as soon as the light came the horrified workers found the lower room in still worse confusion. Boys were banging at the shutters and door, the girls inside shouting and singing, and even fighting, slates, books and sewing being used as missiles; and one or two girls were reading the books at the desk, and finding out who had paid the club money and who not, and other interesting details. One of the ladies went to speak to the lads outside and one threw his cap in and getting his foot in the doorway prevented the door being closed. Remonstrances were of no use. They wished to come in and play 'with the lasses'. At last the cap was thrown out, and the door shut and locked for fear any girl might open it. An attempt was then made to get peace restored, but the boys had taken up the cellar grate outside, had dropped into the dark cellar, groped their way up the steps and three grinning lads emerged through the cellar door into the kitchen amid shrieks of terror from the girls. The ladies greeted them with silence, and locking the door through which they came, put that key too in safety. The boys struck across the kitchen to the outer door and found themselves trapped. They didn't like it. 'Now' said the lady, 'I suppose we must give you incharge for housebreaking. You know what the law has to say to burglars?' (She didn't, but the effect of these was just as impressive.) (Stanley, 1890, p.196)

The ladies who begin with a feeling of sympathy for the girls, and who have themselves a set of high moral values they are concerned to share, find themselves threatening to call the police. In this way, care, concern and control have run hand in hand along the path of charity for more than a century.

Maude Stanley recognised well some of the qualities necessary in workers who will run along that path, for whom her book is written. She advises ladies to start slowly and to give some consideration as to whether the club should be organised on a neighbourhood basis, whether it should be limited by the occupations that the girls are in, and whether it should be linked to a particular church. She makes many useful organisational points early in the book – concerning age groups, the keeping of books, the establishing of a girls' committee – and her book contains what must be one of the earliest discussions of the role of volunteers and paid workers. She stresses the importance of recognising that the role of the philanthropic organisation must have priority over the individual needs of lady helpers , especially over the desire of ladies to be of assistance.

She sees the role of the club as primarily concerned with raising girls' standard of education. The curriculum reflected that provided by the school boards of the time and aimed to provide girls with the means to fulfil their female role, within the context of their station in life. Cooking, needlework, cutting out, laundry and Bible classes formed the staple subjects; singing, dancing and drill supplemented the curriculum.

The first women youth workers

The ladies who help 'must have a dignity in themselves which will command respect' and must be able to encourage a love of learning:

> Our work with many girls is to help them find out their own powers and to raise them more in their own estimation, for if a girl is stupid the fact of being thought so will put out even the small spark of intelligence that remains in her. (Stanley, 1890, p.72)

At the same time, the club may find it necessary to employ a superintendent: a full-time worker who will inevitably become closer to the girls than the ladies of the committee. The question of the class of the superintendent is considered carefully by Maude Stanley, but, in the spirit of cross-class influence which permeated the philanthropic initiatives of the time, she hesitates to opt firmly for the employment of a lady:

> We have had the experience of a lady as superintendent and also one of the same class as the girls and we do not recommend either one or the other as absolutely the best; the essential is to find a woman with great friendliness, love for the girls, warm sympathy, order and liveliness, who will never be tired or rather who will never let her feelings, mental or physical, interfere with the work of the club. (Stanley, 1890, p.31)

This job description for a saint is usually written in more detail now in the 1990s, and with less direct emphasis on personality. Yet Maude Stanley's account contains one of the central elements of a contemporary definition of professionalism: an ability to prioritise the work and the project rather than the worker's own needs, when they are in conflict. Unfortunately, it continues in a vein which is also still all too recognisable, especially when the status of part-time workers who are the majority of the workforce is discussed:

> The salary required for a superintendent will be some consideration when funds are low, but as it will only occupy the evenings of a working woman, a very large pay should not be required. Should the superintendent be a lady, her salary need not be much more, as it would not be wise to engage one who would have to depend on this salary for her maintenance. (Stanley, 1890, p.32)

Maude Stanley clearly intended the girls' clubs to be ruled with scarcely a voice or a salary being raised.

Keeping girls off the streets

Maude Stanley also relished a challenge to her authority. In a chapter dedicated to the discussion of the differences in social position among the work girls, she is not afraid to name them:

> But there are other classes of work girls, factory hands, who after the day's work are always in the street, who are rude, vulgar and boisterous. In one part of London where a girls' club has been established they have been seen on a Saturday night fighting one with another bared to their waists, and yet these, by the gentle and kindly influence of a good matron in a girls' club, have been, may we not say, tamed and civilised. Many of our readers may never have seen the class of girl I now refer to – girls who will roll about the pavement three or four together, their hair cut straight over their foreheads, shawls over their heads, insulting every decent woman they meet; but even these, if they can be brought to the club, may become quiet and well behaved. (Stanley, 1890, p.193)

Keeping girls off the streets was clearly as much on the agenda of the girls' clubs as it was of the lads' clubs in the same era, and the distractions of dancing, drinking and other 'commercial' opportunities were real. Cleaning up the slums, then as now, also meant cleaning out the population of the slums, and yet Maude Stanley speaks warmly of her relationship with the 'wild girls', rather as Baden-Powell would later declare that 'the best sort of boy is the hooligan' (Pearson, 1983). Writing of Newport Market and Princes Row in Soho, Stanley comments:

> These abodes, formerly the possessions of princes, had become so low in their surroundings, that we are thankful they are now swept away with the improvements of Charing Cross Road and Shaftesbury Avenue.
>   The wild girls who used to call themselves the forty thieves, and lived about these courts, and the lads who assumed the like designation, where are they gone to? We see them no longer about Soho. (Stanley, 1890, p.263)

The 1980s: The girls' work movement

Girls' work and the women's liberation movement

Perhaps, a lifetime later, it was the grandchildren of these wild girls who returned, to Soho as well as to many other places, celebrating wildness and power in the name of 'the women's liberation movement' – not off the streets, but on the streets instead. Maude Stanley tamed the wild girls and set them to domestic service. In 1982, girls were writing for themselves in a collection called *Girls are Powerful*, edited by Susan Hemmings at *Spare Rib*, the women's liberation magazine. This collection of lively, aggressive essays found its way onto the shelves of many young women's projects in the 1980s, where women workers were attempting to understand young women's perspective on the world and to work out a new language for talking about discrimination and oppression. This involved a new vocabulary, and the word 'sexism' in particular became shorthand for a whole burgeoning understanding of how women are oppressed.

There are certainly persistent themes from the earlier attention to girls in the 1880s: particularly lack of opportunities for education and employment of a satisfying kind, and the experience of low pay. *Girls are Powerful* contains pieces on hairdressing, babysitting and Saturday shop work. But on the whole, the spirit of the enterprise and the way in which girls are a focus of attention seems quite transformed.

Firstly, this is a collection where young women speak for themselves. No one is going to speak 'on their behalf' or define 'their best interests' for them. Young women who produced the magazine *Shocking Pink* wrote:

> So no matter how much older feminists think it's important to put their energy into young women's projects, girls' nights in youth clubs and so on, it won't work if they see their role as educators. That's a patronising basis, neither equal nor conducive to trust.
>
> What we are saying is that we are already feminists. There are at the moment many hundreds of young women, politically aware and active, defining their sexuality, organising women's groups in schools and colleges, forming bands, starting magazines. Your ageist assumptions deny us our ability to think for ourselves, to create and make our own decisions. In your minds, you place our feminism on another level, below that of yours ... We've all got it hard. We must stop turning it into some kind of competition, and recognise each other's struggles. (Hemmings, 1982, p.155)

Secondly, it is clear that young women's ambitions for change will extend far beyond the conventional definitions of politics into questions of personal life: looks and friendship, the age of consent and lesbianism are as relevant for this collection as educational and employment opportunities.

Thirdly, although many of the pieces do address and express a sense of threat and powerlessness experienced by young women (despite the courageous title), the source of danger is now on the whole understood to be in the workings of an unjust system. The appropriate response is to be found in collective organising. For Maude Stanley, in the 1890s, the dangers facing girls were in the form of dancing, prostitution and drink. Her responses lay in a concern for morality and spirituality, religion and purity. Wider feminist responses in the same period lay, for example, in the agitation to raise the age of consent. By the 1980s, the age of consent rules are defined by girls writing in *Girls are Powerful* as part of the problem. In a reversal of expectations, Asian girls, who are described as 'Growing Angry, Growing Strong', reject the exaggeratedly lady-like passivity to which British culture seems to assign them. Racist and sexist expectations are the problem and the dangers. Organising collectively and speaking on our own behalf are the antidotes.

Early in the 1980s, it seemed as if the agenda for youth work with girls and young women might have shifted, away from the philanthropic focus on girls as problems to girls as people with potential. The sense of excitement and of movement made collective organising as women exciting and exhausting. Accounts of practice in particular settings could always be framed by reference to a wider movement. For example, even as late as 1989, Lena Dominelli and Eileen McLeod could claim that feminist campaigns and networks formed the basis of feminist social work, and that feminist community work could retain an identity not totally incorporated within professional community work (Dominelli and McLeod, 1989, p.46).

In *Feminism for Girls: An Adventure Story*, Trisha McCabe communicated this sense of movement by talking about the differences and arguments among feminists, in a way which current accounts of the movement's history seem to erase:

> With the WLM (Women's Liberation Movement) there are lots of different politics and women put their energy and time into the areas that they see as the most important or relevant to them. We have big disagreements, not to mention rows. Women aren't nice to each other all the time! Our ideas can be so different that it can make it difficult, or impossible, to always work together. And feminists outside of the WLM may have different ideas again. But that doesn't mean that we shouldn't listen to each other or that we aren't all fighting for the same thing. The however-many thousands of women that are involved in the WLM in this country (and there are millions more, in every country of the world) obviously don't agree on how to end women's oppression, or exactly what kind of society we want to build. The WLM is a movement, not a political party or a social set, precisely because it can encompass so many different political positions. The movement has broad aims – not a political programme – and what we have in common is that we all want women's liberation, we all want changes and we all want choices. (McCabe and McRobbie, 1981, p.14)

Girls are Powerful and *Feminism for Girls: An Adventure Story* are books which bridge the gap between a sense of a wider women's liberation movement and the practice of youth and community work which became known as 'the girls' work movement'. Some of the history of this movement, particularly its connection with the Girls' Work Unit at the National Association of Youth Clubs, is recorded in detail in the book written by the NAYC workers who were subsequently made redundant by the NAYC: *Coming in from the Margins: Youth Work with Girls and Young Women* (Carpenter and Young, 1986). I can only offer a brief and very partial snapshot of this recent history here. But it is undoubtedly the spirit of the girls' work movement which informs the rest of this book.

Organisation of women youth workers

In the mid-1970s, projects had begun to develop in London and in Manchester. By the late 1970s, there was pressure on the National Association of Youth Clubs to establish separate events for girls and women. These continued until the mid-1980s, alongside the publication of the *Working with Girls Newsletter*. The events and publications of the Girls' Work Unit became a major resource for the work. The unit was closed very suddenly in 1986, and the actions of the NAYC managers who made the decision to close the unit brought about a nationwide campaign by women workers and their allies in the trade unions to restore the unit, or at least to restore the organisation's support to girls' work. A 'pirate edition' of the *Working with Girls Newletter*, with the cover illustration 'The Grass Roots are Bloomin' Wonderful', appeared on the desk of every committee member who attended the executive meeting which made the decision. Women workers' groups, trade union branches and young women's groups picketed the hotel. Resolutions from regional organisations threatened to disaffiliate and break up the NAYC. All this collective organising was evidence that the movement did not belong to the NAYC, nor even to the Girls' Work Unit.

Two other forms of organising had emerged: the women's caucus within the Community and Youth Worker's Union, in which women had gained the right to organise autonomously within the trade union structure and were using their organising very effectively to promote the interests of women and girls, with a particular focus on promoting the interests of part-time workers; and secondly, the National Organisation for Work with Girls and Young Women (NOWGYW), which was in existence from 1981 to 1994. The original working group for the NOWGYW circulated proposals for a constitution with the following aims in 1980:

Some of the areas which we aim to develop are:

- an information and resources unit
- a network of women youth and community workers
- support for workers who are starting to work with girls in an alternative way
- the initiation of a training programme both for workers and young women

- the acquisition of campsites and residential premises for use by young women's groups
- the setting up of a training college specifically for women youth and community workers.

While many of these aims are very long term, action has been taken on some already. We hope that more clubs, projects and women youth workers' groups will join as soon as possible, so that they will be involved in determining the nature of the organisation from the start. No hard and fast decisions have been made, except to actually get the organisation moving.

The National Organisation for Work with Girls and Young Women could radically change the thinking on girls in the Youth Service. From being seen primarily as a 'problem', they could be recognised as a positive force with a great deal of energy and imagination which, at present, is wasted in most clubs and projects. (NOWGYW, no date, p.4)

Throughout the 1980s, this democratic and autonomous organisation developed strong and active regional organisations. Annual meetings were well attended. The NOWGYW established a small base in Manchester and was able to appoint paid workers. As Michelle Walmsley and Liz Osborne have noted:

At the time it was seen as innovatory to have headquarters outside London or Leicester, but the National Organisation was never afraid to respond to its members' radical and progressive ideas. Indeed, the central debates which took place in the National Organisation were always focused on issues originally seen as marginal by mainstream services but which are now identified as central. The whole notion of 'empowerment' came from the direct practice of women succeeding in raising young women's esteem, confidence and skills so that they were really taking more control of their lives. Today's curriculum has been shaped by these women's ideas, so that service delivery plans now routinely include equal opportunites and monitoring processes to try to ensure that work is directed to previously excluded groups (currently young carers, young lesbians, disabled young women, bisexual young women, mixed race families etc.). (Osborne and Walmsley, 1995, p.3)

The 'Sisters are Doing it for Themselves' young women's conference was organised by members in 1986 and launched the Young Women's Council, enabling young women's participation at the executive level of the organisation.

Sadly, as a result of a sustained attack on the funding of girls' work during the early 1990s, the decision to wind up the NOWGYW was taken at the AGM in Manchester in July 1994. In an essay which documents the history of the NOWGYW, Liz Osborne and Michelle Walmsley point out that the inequalities which the organisation was established in part to address have persisted:

> Work with boys and young men has failed to keep pace with the gains and sheer weight of work achieved by girls and young women's workers in past years. Ironically, whilst the 'B' Team provides some sort of national resource, at least in training and materials, new girls' work resources rarely appear. Indeed, the bright and challenging NAYC 'Girls Can Do Anything' poster set is making a reappearance in some centres – flares and pigtails have gone out of fashion and in again yet nothing comparable is available!
>
> Unlike these images, the means whereby women workers and young women empowered themselves and each other have never 'gone out of fashion'. We continue delivering a 'core curriculum' of work with girls and young women (identifying power and inequalities in our lives; challenging all discrimination and oppression at every level; esteem/confidence building; developing political awareness; anti-sexism; learning to support each other; individual growth through group challenges) with unchanging methods (assertiveness skills; group work; new experiences in a safe setting; peer education; communication skills; inter-agency co-operation etc.) but in more difficult circumstances.
>
> Women workers are used to having to be more active, more accountable than male colleagues. We are often at considerable personal and professional risk through being outspoken, and increasingly women in management positions are made similarly vulnerable.
>
> We hope that a different national body will one day be called for by women workers, building on the history of work with girls and young women once more. (Osborne and Walmsley, 1995, p.9)

Forward to the 1890s?

Self-activity or protection? Risk and challenge/risk and danger

It is clear now, however, that the optimistic energy and activism of the girls' work movement – with its stress on self-activity, risk and challenge – has not yet been sufficiently strong to transform the long-standing agenda of risk and danger with which girls' work has continually been embroiled. Indeed, Maude Stanley would certainly recognise the language spoken in many young women's projects today. The continuities with the philanthropic agenda of the late nineteenth century now seem very strong. Maude Stanley ended her book with a discussion of the danger of overpopulation and the link between overpopulation and poverty:

We are always aiming at improving the education of the masses, we make it possible for the lowest to pass through the primary to the secondary education, we teach the adults by means of lectures within the reach of all. We enable all parishes at their own will to levy a rate, in order to establish free libraries, we look after the health of our population and we establish by means of poor rates excellent hospitals for fevers, smallpox and diphtheria, where the working man gets as perfect treatment, and nursing, as could be given to any in the land.

Countless other schemes are afloat and a vast army of unpaid workers are gallantly doing their utmost to improve our overgrown population; and yet we are never even abreast of the flood, that seems to be always surging around us, of destitution and poverty. And will not all unite in saying that the chief cause of this perplexing difficulty is that of over-population? And is not this evil mostly the result of early marriages? (Stanley, 1890, p.234)

Many projects concerned with work with young women today are framed by the Health of the Nation agenda of reducing teenage pregnancies. Maude Stanley's concern with the dangers of dancing and drinking find their echoes in projects with a drugs education focus, and the distractions of popular culture still seem to challenge the serious educational focus of girls' work.

The sense in Maude Stanley's work that girls on the streets are at continual risk of sexual exploitation finds some echoes in the place occupied by 'the child protection agenda' in work with girls and young women today.

This consistent agenda of seeing girls as 'at risk', in need of protection and appropriate training in becoming a woman is concerned with retaining and shoring up existing class relations and existing relationships between the sexes. It is in itself, a recognisable focus for feminist political activity. The fact that work with girls and young women can shift so readily from an agenda concerned with challenging existing forms of power relationships to an agenda which is essentially rooted in the practice of charity is a matter of concern to a number of practitioners.

The difference between dominant assumptions about 'separate spheres' and autonomous feminist organising as women

In considering this shift, it is useful to pay attention to the links between arguments about separate spheres and arguments about autonomous organising. It is here that the difference made by the principles and aims which underpin practice, rather than by the methods alone, is manifest. It is, after all, perfectly possible and consistent to undertake separate work with girls and women which is not concerned with challenging women's subordination. 'Separate spheres' work is work which enables girls to undertake activities 'appropriate to their station in life' and not to get into too much trouble. Autonomous anti-sexist work is based on the commitment to breaking out of the position of women defined and categorised as persons only when viewed in their relationship with men: as mothers or girlfriends/wives most powerfully, but also as comrades and co-workers. Autonomous work is an assertion that young women are persons, both in their own right and in relation to one another. It therefore provides a powerful potential base from which to recognise and challenge women's subordination.

However, in practical terms, it is quite possible and even likely, that a young women's group engaging in a health and fitness body workshop is not easily distinguished from a girls' club where make-up and beauty sessions are the most popular request. It is the focus, direction and movement of the work which makes the difference: that it moves away from hierarchies, that it moves from the local to the global, that it seeks dialogue and transformation. All these contribute to the power of autonomous work. As well as having different aims and purposes, the role of the worker in autonomous anti-sexist work is seen as different. Alongside the practice of charity comes the development of the patronising attitude of the lady towards the girls. In autonomous work with girls, the worker is positioned in solidarity with the girls and young women she is working with. While not denying differences of role, status and histories, it is essential that commonalities are not denied either, and that both difference and commonality are worked with in the interests of challenging women's subordination. In anti-sexist work, it can be acknowledged that women workers have something to gain as well as something to give in the work they do.

Taking risks and acknowledging difference are sources of creativity and strength

In this book, I am seeking to celebrate some of the 1970s rediscoveries about autonomy, self-activity and collective action. I also attempt to locate current practice in relation to those ideologies of risk and danger which date back at least a century and which still frame dominant social thinking about girls and young women. In moving from oppressive constructions of sameness to an attention to difference not as a threat to unity, but as a promise of greater strength, it has been the work of Black women which has often pointed the way. At the very beginning of the work of the Girls' Work Unit at the NAYC, the research undertaken by Laxmi Jamdagni and commissioned by the Department of Education and Science was a focus for this shift. It offered an early challenge to women workers to address the links between the identification of 'difference' and 'risk' and the exercise of power.

Having chosen to focus attention on Asian girls, Laxmi Jamdagni writes:

> My aim in the groups was to provide the girls with the opportunity to talk about their experience of being Asian girls in Britain. Whilst they often need to talk through with me some of the problems they faced as girls in relation for example to their families, the specific focus of my research was to challenge the stereotyped notions of Asian girls being 'at risk' per se – a view popularly held by white professional workers including those who designed this project. (Jamdagni, 1980, p.3)

Like Laxmi Jamdagni, I wish to question those ideologies of risk, danger and protection. I would like to reassociate the idea of 'risk' with excitement, rebellion, wildness, pleasure and potential. Like Maude Stanley, but with a quite opposite purpose, I shall ask: 'Where are the wild girls now?'

3 The principles of practice: Empowerment and autonomy

Work with girls and young women is still widely regarded with scepticism and mistrust, and where good practice exists it is due almost entirely to women workers who are challenging the system and offering to young women a curriculum of relevant social education in an environment where they feel confident and secure. (DES, WO and NACYS, 1989, p.6)

Kate Clements, the youth and community worker responsible for the development of the Girls' Work Unit in Lancashire, tells an important story. She was appointed to her full-time post just as the Girls' Work Unit at the National Association of Youth Clubs was being closed down. One of her first 'official appointments' in her new post was to attend the demonstration which had been called in Leicester to coincide with the meeting where a decision about the Girls' Work Unit was to be taken. The banners that were flying and the crowd of women and men who gathered seemed, both then and now, to mark a turning point. For the Girls' Work Unit at NAYC, it was a full stop. For the Girls' Work Unit in Lancashire, the banners were heralding a beginning.

There were six girls' groups in Lancashire then. Now there are 66. Work with girls persists despite its often reported demise. New generations of workers become involved and ask the same basic questions: 'Why should we work with girls, and what sort of work should we do?' The basic concepts which underpin the work need to be stated and discussed over and over again.

The aim of this chapter is to present and discuss some key concepts and the thinking behind them, so that the conceptual framework which underpins community-based education with girls and young women can continue to be developed and to change.

The debate about empowerment

A commitment to empowerment is often claimed to unify the practice of community-based, informal education work with girls and young women. However, the term seems elastic and capable of such a wide range of reference as to be of doubtful usefulness. Rather than give up on the struggle to define its meaning however, I will offer here a specific perspective on empowerment which derives from feminist analysis. In doing this, I intend to shift the terms of the debate away from what seems to me to be a fruitless and mistaken polarisation between individual and structural accounts of power.

Many writers on the question of 'empowerment' draw a sharp distinction between approaches which seem to be based in an individualistic model of self-help and the consumer movement, and those which are based in a collective model of resistance to structures of oppression. This distinction is drawn particularly sharply by David Ward and Audrey Mullender:

> Broadly, empowerment is associated at one end of a continuum with the New Right's welfare consumerism and at the other with the user movement which demands a voice in controlling standards and services themselves. One is 'the essential expression of individualism'; the other rests on a collective voicing of universal need. (Ward and Mullender, 1992, p.21)

They argue that it is only on the basis of a clear analysis of the structural nature of oppression that community work practice can promote empowerment. This commitment to a structural analysis of power relations is clearly a necessary antidote to the 'power to the people' rhetoric of free-market Conservative social policy, in which the power of the citizen is her purchasing power: her ability to choose to buy or not to buy certain services.

These two versions of empowerment do represent different political orientations to welfare. However, from the point of view of a feminist analysis of power relations, the distinction between the individual and the structural creates a mistaken framework which separates the personal from the political. This individual/structural dichotomy prevents an analysis of the social, and prevents the recognition that all power, even when it is exercised by individuals, derives from the social order. Even the physical force of the natural world, even the apparent domain of spiritual power (the realm of angels and archangels!) can be analysed most convincingly as power when it is exercised through the social domain.

Power

The most general definitions of power build on the account given by Max Weber: 'to achieve one's will, even against the resistance of others' (quoted in Lukes, 1986, p.2). David Beetham gives this account:

In its widest sense, the power a person has indicates their ability to produce intended effects upon the world around them, to realise their purposes within it, whatever their purposes happen to be. Power in this general sense depends upon certain preconditions: the presence of personal capacities or powers, such as health, strength, knowledge and skill; the possession of material resources; and space or scope, in the sense of freedom from control, obstruction or subservience to the purposes of others. (Beetham, 1991, p.43)

Power is socially organised

Other theorists have emphasised that the definition of power needs to be social from the very start. Hannah Arendt argued that:

> Power corresponds to the human ability not just to act but to act in concert. Power is never the property of an individual; it belongs to a group and remains in existence only so long as the group keeps together. (Arendt, 1986, p.64)

On this basis, when individuals hold and exercise power, they are able to do so only because it is socially sanctioned. Power is invested in individuals by groups, and can be removed from them. So the expression 'power to the people' is profoundly misleading. Power belongs to the people and derives from the people. It is only ever lent to rulers, and it can be re-claimed. Rulers can be overthrown. Power relations can be reconstructed.

Power is channelled through socially-sanctioned relations of domination and subordination

Power is unequally distributed, and it flows through channels and relationships which are structured in patterns of dominance and subordination. These are systematic and continuous relations whereby one group defines and limits the power of another group, legitimately and in order to achieve the purposes of society. The problem for the subordinate group is that the dominant group has the power to define what are legitimate forms of domination. There are a number of means to power, which can provide the basis of these social relations. To be dominant means to possess these means to power and to exclude others from them. Power relations operate through processes of possession and exclusion.

What are the means to power?

Many social theorists have identified the following aspects of social life as key aspects of power relations. Firstly, there is the possession of or exclusion from material resource: on the one hand, the means of life – such as food, water, clothing and all other material goods; on the other hand, the means of death – the capacity to control and use physical force destructively. Secondly, there is control of socially necessary activities and the possession of skills associated with their performance: this includes the whole area of the division of labour and the reproduction of life and new generations, as well as caring for the sick and the dying. Thirdly, power is invested in positions of command and in the ability to generate the rules of social life and of legality. Fourthly, power is invested in the work of naming and defining the aims and purposes of society: it is educative, cultural and moral.

These aspects of power exist in all societies, and it is through the social relations of exclusion and possession that domination is secured.

Power and discourse: The productive capacities of power

Writers and theorists following the work of Michel Foucault have stressed that all the power systems analysed above have a discursive aspect. (Foucault, 1980). They are all concerned with naming, defining and bringing into being particular kinds of subjectivities as well as with laying down principles of exclusion. In this account, power is creative as well as regulatory, and it always involves the possibilities of resistance.

Because of its attention to subjectivities and because of the way in which accounts of discursive formations enable resistances to domination to be described and analysed, Foucauldian perspectives have been very attractive to feminists.

Feminist accounts of power

There is a diversity of accounts of power which name themselves feminist, but they all share a project of analysing domination and subordination, with a particular attention to the way power is distributed in the social relations between men and women.

Feminist analyses of power and resistance attempt to uncover the ways in which power flows through gender relations, and to offer an alternative account, which counters women's subordination. So, feminist analysis addresses the means of power when it considers the gendering of wealth and poverty. It addresses questions of power when it considers the gendering of coercion, the control of the means of physical force and violence, as well as questions of how the power of the body is expressed in sexuality. It addresses questions of power when it addresses questions of the sexual division of labour, particularly issues of reproduction and mothering, and care for the sick or frail.

Feminist analysis considers the 'relations of ruling': the gendering of access to positions of control and command, related to the practice of government, but also to the control and command of major social organisations. Finally, feminist analysis of power is concerned with the practices of naming, defining and debating the aims, purposes and values of society, with sources of cultural and educative power.

Working with girls and young women in community settings can best be understood as empowering when it engages with one or more of these aspects of power. So, empowering practice may be about addressing the problems of poverty or understanding the nature of women's access to wealth. It may be about creating places of safety where women can build up strategies for resisting or escaping violence. It may be about exploring the responsibilities of motherhood, or of 'community care' for other dependants. It may be about enabling young women to explore their own sexualities. It may be about making connections into society-wide democratic processes, or connecting with other points of control or command, such as the legal system: encouraging those who make the rules to change the rules to the benefit of women. Finally, empowering practice is almost always about participating in a process of naming and defining the issues for public debate, rather than accepting the definitions of the dominant discourses. It is for this reason that a commitment to separate and autonomous work with women, which excludes men, remains a vital strategy. Women, like men, can exercise power by rules of exclusion. Women, as subordinates, are often unaccustomed to exercising and naming this power to act. In exercising the power to exclude men from groups, women turn the tables on the dominant group, and in this, setting new agendas can be rehearsed and can emerge.

I am arguing that to term a practice 'empowering' is not to refer to a particular method, but to its purpose and direction. Nor does feminist practice encompass only one dimension: only counselling and support, or only networking, or only campaigning. Different projects will participate in different aspects of the feminist project at different times. The same project will change in its emphasis and orientation. No one project can participate in all the work of empowerment, and different alliances will be forged at different times. Often, it will be the educative and discursive aspects of power that are addressed; less frequently, the work on poverty, or the division of labour. Sometimes projects will engage with the work of providing a safe base in relation to violence or sexuality. At other times, they will be able to join in campaigns which address the legal and political system. What matters is that projects identify how their methods and aims and work agendas participate in a feminist project of empowerment.

Because the structure of power relations between men and women is very much imbricated in the public/private divide, male dominance and female subordination is secured by rendering many of the public concerns of women as 'private' or 'personal'. Feminism challenges the form currently taken by the public/private divide. But feminist practice also works at both sides of that divide. It is for this reason that feminists must acknowledge the process of empowerment as both personal and structural.

Empowerment is personal

Empowerment involves a personal process of making choices, taking responsibility, acknowledging potential, recognising the barriers to the fulfilment of that potential. In the case of work with girls and young women, this involves developing a curriculum which is concerned with enabling choice within personal relationships – especially, perhaps, sexual relationships, discussion of the meanings of motherhood and daughterhood and practical support in relation to contraception, abortion and/or the positive commitment to children. Questions about employment and economic independence can be explored, and personal and group strategies for understanding and tackling poverty can be developed. It involves a recognition of the existence of violence, harassment and the possibility of abuse in various forms in the lives of young women. It means raising questions about dependency and independence, the strengths that can be gained from relationships with others, and the constraints that the same network of relationships, the same 'community', can impose. This person-centred approach to empowerment constantly confronts the question of self-confidence, confidence-building and motivation. Lack of power leads to lack of confidence, and thereby to inertia.

A primary aim, expressed over and over again in professional reports, is the building up of self-confidence. Self-confidence is built up in a number of ways, but they each involve careful attention to the particular young women who are participating in a project, their particular interests and strengths, as well as their particular difficulties. Being on the receiving end of personal attention can, in itself, boost confidence enormously. Workers have often used methods drawn from assertiveness training to enable young women to have more confidence in defining small steps which can be taken to improve their situation, to rehearse different strategies for handling relationships, and to help young women think about their own needs as well as their children's or the needs of other dependants. A good deal of the practice is about encouraging self-reflection by young women, encouraging a sense of 'life-scripts' and autobiographies, seeing young women as potentially 'authors of their own lives' and also encouraging awareness of how life-stories interconnect.

Offering new opportunities and challenges is also a common method of building up self-confidence: as young women try new activities, they grow in confidence to tackle new ways of living that are within their grasp. Such new activities can include survival activities, such as cooking on a low budget, or joining a credit union to help in the management of debt, or learning basic health measures (such as fertility awareness, early pregnancy testing or the practice of 'safer sex'). New activities can also be opportunities for personal enjoyment and development: taking part in sporting or drama or arts activities is a common method of working. This can extend to opportunities to join formal education programmes and opportunities to take part in political campaigning and advocacy.

The point is that programme-planning derives from a combination of the skills and areas of interest of workers and a careful attention to the personal stories of the girls and young women who make up the groups the project works with. The aim is to build up pride, motivation and self-confidence among girls and young women who have been denied the opportunity to develop these. This work of enabling young women to build up a sense of pride and confidence in themselves as women can occur in every setting.

Empowerment is structural

A structural emphasis often addresses the organisational and 'command' aspects of power. Its origins are in democratic traditions of community work practice which focus on making power structures and bureaucracies accountable to the people they are supposed to assist. It is the process of 'making public' hitherto private troubles that matters. Empowerment is the process of struggle for definition of those troubles within, and often against, the agenda-setting processes and definitions of the currently powerful.

Examples of empowerment in practice can be relatively small-scale. A project might invite a speaker from a feminist organisation such as Women's Aid; it might encourage young women to analyse advertisements and take part in a public debate about the representation of women.

On a slightly wider scale, young women's projects have been involved in establishing resource centres and libraries which give young women access to the debates about their position in society, and projects have run literacy programmes and publishing projects which enable young women to voice their own perspectives on contemporary politics. Larger initiatives, embracing national and international campaigns, have remained a persistent feature of practice in some projects: such as, in 1994, campaigns about the Child Support Agency, in support of young women affected by immigration and asylum legislation, or against cutbacks in Section 11 funding (Section 11 of the Local Government Act 1966 was the result of widespread debate during the mid-1960s about the impact of migration on particular localities, and was intended as a way of distributing central government money to local authorities in order to help meet the special needs of ethnic minority groups in relation to education and social welfare (Solomos, 1993, p.103)). Young women's projects have organised to make public bodies such as health authorities, schools and the Youth Training Scheme more girl-friendly. Links have been made with user movements, particularly in the field of mental health, which challenge the role of 'experts' in defining the nature of and solutions to mental health problems.

In such campaigning activity, young women's groups have become part of wider women's networks and campaigns at a national and international level.

Empowerment is social

From an explicit feminist perspective, Sandra Butler and Claire Wintram (1991) distinguish between feminist group work and political and community action. They see dangers in focusing empowerment on political and community action: that women are asked yet again to prioritise the needs of others before their own selves. In *Feminist Groupwork*, they explore some of the processes of collective action, which draw on a prioritising of women's selves in feminist group work:

> Individual power, stemming from a positive attitude towards Self, precipitates collectivity. Collective action which involves sublimation of the Self becomes a training in conformity in the name of a sense of belonging. The last thing a women's group wants to do is provide yet another source of social pressure for women, in which the words may be different but the song remains the same. (Butler and Wintram, 1991, p.152)

These writers are very aware of the problematic nature of personal and social change which can be precipitated by feminist group work, including the potential for an increase in women's sense of frustration and helplessness as our consciousness of our own rights grows. As they say:

> The implications of personal and social change while occupying a position of economic and social dependence are great. (Butler and Wintram, 1991, p.158)

At the same time, they argue that a shift in focus is possible, once women begin to prioritise themselves and other women:

> The motivation for social change is that women are fighting for other women, and this proves to be a major turning point for group members who habitually act on behalf of families and children. Women in poverty have no legitimate socially granted power to determine their own fate economically, socially or politically. Yet through membership of the group, women can bring about anything that is within their grasp by placing each other centre stage. (Butler and Wintram, 1991, p.159)

It is within this tension between 'what is within our grasp' and 'what remains outside our power' that much of the most creative work with girls and young women occurs. The distinction between women's lack of legitimate, socially-granted power to act as women on our own behalf and the empowering possibilities of small women's groups to assist in 'bringing about what is within our grasp' is a very helpful one. It prevents absurd claims being made on behalf of particular projects or moments in small group work: small groups of women who are in positions of dependency facing big power structures do remain dependent and structurally oppressed. However, it also enables a challenge to purely functionalist accounts of power systems: the creativity of a small group is already a place where change and challenge to women's subordination occurs. We do not have to wait until 'after the revolution' or for the election of the next reforming government.

Feminist insight into the links between the personal and the political offers a way beyond the polarity of 'individual' and 'collective' approaches to empowerment. No one who has shared the energy of young women at the end of a residential weekend focusing on confidence-building or assertiveness, perhaps using some very traditional youth work approaches to outdoor education, will doubt that young women's sense of achievement and worth is empowering. The group may never meet again as a group, and yet young women are taking a belief in themselves and their own potential with them which will conflict with the far too low expectations they encounter.

One of the most frequently-used 'work books' for work with girls and young women is entitled *Greater Expectations* (Szirom and Dyson, 1986). The work of raising expectations already participates in a movement of resistance. However, such work alone is easily marginalised and re-packaged as a form of individualism: 'You can do it if you really want.' It can then pathologise those who fail to take initiatives, fail to take up the opportunities offered. Confidence-building work needs to link to public debate and dialogue with those organisations and practices which destroy young women's confidence and limit or lower their expectations. It is the practice of small group work which can provide that link and ensure that feminist practice does not disappear into individualism.

Links between women who work in informal education and allies within major social institutions are very important. For example, a project which was established to explore the levels of use of the contraceptive Depo Provera among young women in a particularly poor neighbourhood began by focusing on the problems which young women presented to the medical profession and the qualities in the young women which led them to being seen as unreliable contraceptive-users and therefore likely to be prescribed Depo Provera. However, it soon became apparent that it was perhaps more useful to explore the attitudes of doctors and other medical professionals in the area. Empowerment for young women in relation to contraceptive choice is only partly a matter of young women's own self-confidence. It also depends critically on a public debate which informs the decision-making of medical professionals in this area (Ronan, 1994).

The personal is political

Analyses of power that locate the sources of power only in the economy ('the market') or in formal legal and democratic processes ('the State') neglect some significant aspects of domination and regulation. In the case of the regulation of girls and young women, our bodies and our identities are a central site of power play – whether through the control of our fertility, or through sexual violence, through our relationship with food, or in the manipulation of our body image, including our perception of our skin colour, by the beauty industry.

Power relations operate not only through the market and the economy, but also run right through us, in the social construction of the self. Sometimes, it can seem that what is most personal – in modern societies is most intensely the focus of domination and regulation, and especially so for women, who for long periods have been seen as belonging most closely to the private, domestic and personal sphere. Feminist analyses of the workings of power relationships challenge these separations of the private and the public realms on which liberal political theory depends.

The major social institutions such as schools, hospitals and clinics, churches, mosques, temples and synagogues, the press and broadcasting companies, which themselves challenge the division between personal and public, are increasingly understood as exercising power in their own right, not simply reflecting power relationships produced elsewhere (in the factory or the courtroom, for example), but productive in their own specific ways of domination, subordination and resistance.

To put it another way, the work of 'empowerment' that engages with young women's relationship to schools and to the YTS or to the health care system can no longer be viewed as 'secondary' to the real struggle which is occurring elsewhere. Young women's access to social and cultural power is as important as young women's access to economic and political power. These forms of power are identifiable and different, and not necessarily connected by a hierarchy of power, from base to superstructure. They are aspects of power in a material, historical matrix. Change in any aspect of this matrix of power relationships will affect the whole.

These understandings of the exercise of power also rely on a recognition of the power of language in social relations. The power to name and define is understood as a significant aspect of power relations, and the commitment to processes of 'finding a voice' among subordinate groups are a direct recognition of this power in language.

All this means, in effect, that matters hitherto regarded as 'personal' or 'private' can now be acknowledged as social and potentially in the public domain, and open to public discussion and debate. It also allows us to recognise that the apparent 'lack of self-confidence' of many young women may be a result of social processes which render young women either invisible, or visible only as problems to be regulated, and that therefore, any attempt to build self-confidence is, at least potentially, an act of resistance within existing power relationships.

Feminist analysis and analysing 'the matrix of domination'

The work of the African-American feminist Patricia Hill Collins is helpful in arguing that people resist and experience oppression on the level of personal biography, on the group or community level and at the systemic level of social institutions. She develops the idea of a 'matrix of domination' to explore the complexities of oppression and domination. She suggests that approaches which prioritise one aspect of domination:

> fail to recognise that a matrix of domination contains few pure victims or oppressors. (Hill Collins, 1991, p.229)

> A broader focus stresses the interlocking nature of oppressions that are structured on multiple levels, from the individual to the social structural, and which are part of a larger matrix of domination. Adhering to this inclusive model provides the conceptual space needed for each individual to see that she or he is both a member of multiple dominant groups and a member of multiple subordinate groups. (Hill Collins, 1991, p.230)

In this perspective, personal and collective empowerment are intrinsically linked. Personal fulfilment as a goal is insufficient. Feminist movement is not primarily a movement for self-fulfilment, but a movement for justice. It may indeed involve some short-term sacrifices by some women (including those many women who have chosen to put defending girls' work before their own careers, and sometimes before their own employment). Working out the appropriate methods by which the connections between the personal, the social and the political can be established is a difficult task, especially as women have so often been that place of connection for others.

However, the sense that processes which increase women's sense of our own value can overflow into movements which protest the injustice of treatment which other women receive has a concrete embodiment in the existence of national and international feminist publications, campaigns and organisations. Groups which enable female friendships to develop can also enable connections to be made outside the group within a community or neighbourhood, and alliances to be formed between women who occupy different public or structural roles. This question of alliance is vital, and it is through alliance that community work with girls and young women links to movements for justice.

However, feminism is a movement for justice which embraces as much self-fulfilment and joy as it can. It is good to remember the excitement and pleasure of the work: young women free to dance together without inhibition; the girl abseiling down a rock face to the delight of her friends and to her own delight; willingness to trust from the girl who feels safe to speak about her experience of abuse; 'falling in love' in the young lesbian group; the end to the suicide threats; the celebration of the Eid disco; young women confronting the local government officer about resources for children on the estate; 'saying no' to drugs and dealing as the only option for their children; refusal of sex without condoms, the young women who embark on engineering degrees, and, accompanying it all, the laughter that means we can imagine and understand that the world might change for the better.

The principle of autonomy: Work with girls and women, for girls and women, controlled by girls and women

Much practice now occurs in projects and groups from which boys and men are excluded, and the principle of separate and autonomous provision is very well established in practice. This is often referred to as 'separate work'. The term 'separate work' can easily be taken to mean no more than work in which only girls participate. However, from the point of view of practice which advocates feminism, the term has a stronger meaning. It suggests the independence of girls and women from boys and men, and a commitment to enable girls and women to set and control the agenda. 'Separate work' is attempting to be autonomous work, and the act of excluding men from groups is an act in the direction of empowerment.

Of course, the autonomy of girls' work is usually profoundly circumscribed by organisational hierarchies and the control of funding. Nevertheless, it is now widely recognised that the dynamic of work from which boys and men are excluded is very different and potentially more creative than the dynamic of working with girls as part of mixed groups. It may well be appropriate sometimes for particular girls and boys to work together, but if such mixed work is undertaken on the basis of the experience of separate girls' groups, girls will join the negotiations in mixed groups from a position of greater strength.

Acceptance of the need for 'separate space' unites women whose analyses of the nature of women's subordination differ. For some women, the commitment to separate space is tactical and temporary. For others, it is strategic and very long-term. And for others again, it is visionary and prefigurative of an alternative form of community. All these positions share a recognition that separate space can provide a basis from which male dominance can be understood, negotiated and resisted. New possibilities can emerge when women meet in the absence of men and are temporarily released from the need to act as 'relative creatures'.

Some characteristic explanations given by workers who choose to work separately with women and girls include the following:

- it offers girls the opportunity to meet without pressure from boys and men;
- it offers girls the opportunity to build up and value female friendship and mutual support;
- it enables the creation of a safe environment in which self-confidence can develop and new skills can be tested;
- it enables the creation of an environment in which silences can be broken and difficult, challenging questions explored.

In addition, the following community-based rationales are offered:

- it offers girls the opportunity to do work that is appropriate to women's role in the community;
- it provides the opportunity to do work that is seen as appropriate by religious and community organisations;
- it facilitates the welfare of the whole community.

Within and between these statements, there are a number of potentially conflicting positions. For example, a growth of self-confidence and individual ambition in a young woman may endanger her role as someone who works to facilitate the welfare of the whole community. The exploration of difficult and challenging questions may mean that the work ceases to be 'appropriate' in the eyes of the organisations, be they religious or not, who are sponsoring the work. Autonomous work always raises the question of 'in whose interests?'. There is a tension between promoting young women's rights as individuals and promoting young women's interests as members of communities. Separate, autonomous work can explore what is possible for young women as individuals and what is at stake for them in their membership of communities.

In some projects, the exclusion of men has been a formal policy position. In others, the exclusion of men derives from a commitment to working within the existing friendship and community networks and giving priority to work around young women's own identified concerns. Women's projects in working-class communities, including projects which have focused on work with Asian women and projects which have worked with women of African and African-Caribbean descent, have been strong when they have recognised and drawn on the strength and resourcefulness of women in those communities. In some neighbourhoods, work with girls and young women can build on the achievements of the earlier generation, particularly among Black women who focused on building up voluntary organisations and self-help networks, in the face of the racism of the 'host' community. Working with young women, in this perspective, involves more than a resistance to male dominance. Release from subordination for women in poor communities has never been only a matter of tackling 'the sexual Toryism of men'. It becomes rooted in a practice of resistance to oppression, which includes male dominance, but in which men may sometimes be allies. And it affirms women's already well-developed strengths and capacities for survival. Autonomous work needs to be understood as work which challenges all patterns of dominance, including sexism, but not confined to it.

The principles underlying separate and autonomous work with women need to be explored and discussed each time a project is established and each time links between projects are proposed and alliances suggested. In this way, some of the tensions of the practice can be explored and the work strengthened. It is possible to recognise ahead some of the tensions which may need to be confronted.

Autonomy and young women's rights: The tension between 'autonomy' and 'relationship'

The tension between the need for girls' groups to be separate and autonomous and the need to recognise and debate the place of women within communities of women and men is represented within separate groups in the question of the particular aims of informal education with girls and young women.

Underlying much feminist practice in which girls are offered opportunities for development is a commitment to young women's development as persons in their own right, of equal worth and dignity to men and boys, and with the potential to create their own perspectives in social and political education.

At the same time, young women can be viewed as essentially co-operators and community-builders: the cornerstone from which everything else develops. And the liberal, individualist perspective inherent in the commitment to 'rights' is regarded as inadequate to promote the well-being of young women, which must be a collective enterprise. On the one hand, to become adult means to become an autonomous person, with rights. In the language of developmental psychology, autonomy is seen as a developmental goal for girls as well as for boys. On the other hand, to become an adult means being prepared to take up adult duties and responsibilities. And for women, whose subordinate status means that such access to adulthood is always open to question, both points of view about what it means to be an adult will certainly be questioned in the process of challenging women's subordination.

Many women working in informal education have identified the small group and working through relationships as a method not only for good educational practice, but as an alternative forum where such questions – and in particular the tension between rights and community – can be addressed by young women. Small group work can enable both the recognition of the reality and importance of relationship and the differing life-stories of the individuals who form the groups. Earlier, in relation to empowerment, it was argued that small group work enables women to explore both 'what is within our grasp' and 'what is outside our power'. The focus for working with and through relationships on which small group work depends mean that these questions can be addressed both by individuals and collectively. If relationships become a focus for small group work, as is often the case, then the group work can focus on a number of potential relationships:

- relationships between different girls;
- relationships between young women and older women, particularly sisters, mothers and grandmothers, and cousins and aunts;
- relationships with fathers and brothers;
- relationships with young men, including boyfriends and children's fathers;
- relationships with professional workers such as health visitors, teachers, social workers and GPs who have an impact on their lives and who are 'gatekeepers' of enormous power;
- relationships between neighbourhoods;
- relationships with political representatives;
- relationships between communities in different nations.

It is these relationships which form most of the curriculum for informal education with girls and young women.

Most young women's projects effectively combine in practice an orientation towards the development of individuals and an orientation towards social change. It is important to be able to identify the primary orientation of any project, for projects to be able to shift from one orientation to another, and for projects to be able to make links with one another on the basis of discussions of differences and similarities in interpretation of the term 'empowerment'. The following examples illustrate, I think, the ways in which two projects with different initial orientations both addressed aspects of women's subordination and resistance.

The Hag Fold Project seemed to have a strong orientation to the achievements of particular young women; the Youth Support Project's orientation seemed to focus on engaging with the organisational or 'command' aspects of power. Both made connections, but in different ways, between the lives of the particular young women the projects were established to work with and an analysis of society-wide power relations.

The Hag Fold Young Women's Centre

In the context of Wigan Youth Service's commitment to young people's rights, the workers at Hag Fold Young Women's Centre, Poddy Peerman and Julia Keenan, expressed their aims in the following ways.

Within the constraints of the budget, Hag Fold Young Women's Centre aims to:

1   provide an environment that challenges oppression within society;
2   ensure that the physical environment of the project is conducive to all women;
3   increase young women's confidence and stimulate personal development;
4   encourage young women to learn to value themselves and other young women;
5   increase young women's knowledge of their rights and the political climate in which they live;
6   increase young women's expectations of their rights and goals;
7   help young women understand what blocks them from having control;
8   enable young women to make informed choices;
9   support young women making changes in their lives.

The workers then went on to express these aims in terms of what they hoped the outcomes for young women who participated in the project might be. They hoped that young women would:

1   take up training opportunities inside and outside the project (e.g. enrolling for courses at the local college; learning to use the word-processor at the centre);
2   take up Youth Service opportunities (e.g. taking driving lessons through the borough-wide driving scheme; going on senior members' training course; joining the Young People's HIV Education Project);

3   take up new opportunities of all types (e.g. one young woman went into car mechanics; several women tried 'fantasy' activities like windsurfing and abseiling);
4   feel valuable and be prepared to consider their own needs (e.g. learning to leave their child in the creche for two hours so as to have space; thinking about what they want from a relationship);
5   gain knowledge and skills for self-development and to aid employment prospects (e.g. overcoming agoraphobia and being able to come out of the house and mix with others; developing tolerance for the opinions of others; e.g. a young woman herself become a youth worker; women developing marketable skills like sewing, typing, welding, childcare);
6   experience the benefits (and difficulties) of collective working and team work (e.g. organising fundraising activities together; campaigning; group discussions and support);
7   challenge put-downs of women, themselves and others;
8   become analytical/more aware about their child-rearing;
9   learn about discrimination and prejudice and the position of oppressed groups;
10   direct their anger in appropriate ways in order to effect change (e.g. a young woman challenging her partner about their behaviour and setting an ultimatum that demands change; complaining to a local councillor about their dissatisfaction with a local service; campaigning to save the project);
11   be involved in making decisions about the life of the project (e.g. via the structure of centre meetings). (Peerman and Keenan, 1993)

The Youth Support Project

The Youth Support Project is a Manchester-based voluntary organisation which has worked mainly but not exclusively with young women. Reflecting on the prospects for improving young women's health by improving their diets (the link between ill health and poverty being as clear as ever), the project workers turned their attention to the fact that local stores were stocking poor-quality produce and selling products which were past their expiry date. They called on their local MP to lobby national food organisations, the National Consumer Council and the Health Inspectorate, as well as the Agriculture Minister, and used the national media to good effect, including the BBC *Watchdog* programme.

In the same year, the project was involved in Women's Action for Benefits, a campaign linked to a nationwide campaign against Social Security cuts. The group organised a conference 'to examine the current position of women within the benefits system, to share information and discuss campaign strategies for the future. The Youth Support Project ran a workshop on maternity benefits. It was well attended. Overall, the conference attracted 120 women. Speakers from the Child Poverty Action Group and Jo Richardson MP were well received.

As the project workers noted in their report: 'As a high percentage of Project users are women claiming benefits this campaign is particularly relevant to them' (Youth Support Project, 1986).

Characteristics of feminist practice

Since 1986, there has been something of a decline in campaigning, and the attempt to turn 'private troubles into public issues' or the desire to turn 'cases into issues, issues into movements' has taken different forms. The long period of Conservative rule in Britain has led to a loss of confidence in what were well-established forms of collective advocacy and collective action. This alone – along with the stress on identifying 'outcomes' so necessary for the funding of projects in the 1990s – may account for the differences in orientation.

As I have already stated, a commitment to empowerment unifies this practice of community-based informal education with girls and young women. The debate about the meanings of empowerment needs to be explicit and engaged with regularly whenever work is established or reviewed. It is possible to offer, at this stage, a statement of some characteristics which seem to inform feminist-inspired informal education practice with girls and young women. This summary should be read as open to change, critique and modification on the basis of continuing debate.

These are some characteristics of feminist practice in informal education with girls and young women.

- There is a commitment to autonomy – the desire to see girls and young women have the opportunity to develop as subjects of their own lives, rather than merely as the objects of professional intervention. There is a recognition of the shared and distinct experiences of adult women workers and of young women in relation to the goal of autonomy, in particular in exploring, from different perspectives and ages, the meaning of 'adult status' for women.

- There is a commitment to openness – this does not exclude the possibility of working with closed groups, or working with women who have been referred to a project. It does, however, mean that young women are to be free to participate or not. It also means that there is positive encouragement for new and different groups of women to participate. There is development and change within the project.

- The work of the project entails active participation – doing and being – by girls and young women. They are not merely consumers, but also creators. Characteristically, the work of informal educators starts from the strengths and concerns of participants, rather than from an already fixed curriculum.

- There is negotiation of the project's programme and agenda of work. Workers or funders are not able alone to define the agenda, goals and purposes of a programme. Young women are critically involved in the development of the project (though not necessarily 'burdened' with management in the name of empowerment). There is a continuous dialogue about the work of the project that 'starts where young women are at, but does not end there'.

- The approach to the work is informal, flexible and not geared to assessment. It is evaluated in relation to its process as much as its end results. Its subject matter is developed from key themes in the lives of young women. Its methods draw on oracy, literacy, arts education, outdoor education and community action, and they link to the school-based curriculum of social and personal education, as well as to women's studies in adult education. It is not subject to assessment at age 7, 11, 16 or older, but the achievements of young women within the frameworks it offers can be recognised and recorded.

- The work uses the methods of social group work and collective action to build on individual young women's strengths and to turn 'private troubles into public issues'. The focus of group work is enjoyment, association, education and community development, as distinct from therapeutic group work. However, it also recognises the need to provide support, both material and emotional, to individuals.

- There is a commitment to making connections with other women's projects and with other projects who share these principles in some degree and are engaged with empowerment/anti-oppressive practice. There is a recognition that women workers, as well as young women who are participants in the work, have much to gain from such initiatives.

4 How to do it

Definitions of youth and community work

Students undertaking initial training courses in youth and community work are often asked, as part of the assessment of their professional practice, how their work differs from that of a social worker or a teacher. They very often reply that they, unlike the others, start from young people's own agenda. They may also reply that youth work or informal education is characterised more by method than by content. Such professional boundary-marking probably disguises more than it reveals, and in the case of youth and community work, it certainly has a compensatory flavour. Unlike social workers and teachers, youth workers exercise absolutely no statutory authority. The compensation for this lack of authority is a whole sphere of influence, exercised through voluntary relationships and enjoyment. No wonder relationships between professionals from these different disciplines can be difficult.

Following the establishment of the first training courses for professional, full-time youth and community workers, there was a period of protracted debate and definition of the professional role. This process of debate and definition is still continuing, and feminist practice has much to contribute. However, it is important to recognise from the outset that this long period of professionalisation has led to a number of shared understandings and agreements about the nature of good practice in informal social education and in community work.

At the same time as this process of professional clarification has been occurring, youth and community work has suffered from a lack of funding and of appropriate resourcing. Much of the resources consist of buildings which constantly require repairs, are difficult to staff, need constant caretaking, and which seem to lend themselves to activities more appropriate to the social containment of boys than to the social and political education of girls or boys. Staff working in such buildings often find themselves policing the building rather than forming educative relationships with young people.

It is these inherent difficulties which have led to a lack of understanding from the formal sector of schooling and from the statutory casework-orientated social services, and which have, until recently, made relationships between feminists working in these different sectors more difficult than they need be.

Recent statements of professional values and activity

In the context of developing appropriate training for both full-time and part-time youth workers, and in the process of professionalisation of community work, there have been a number of codifications of the values and activities which inform good practice. Recent statements of shared principles and values and of the key functions undertaken by youth and community workers have been usefully synthesised by Dr Michael Erault and Dennis Kelly of the University of Sussex in a report commissioned by the National Youth Agency and the Department of Employment.

Erault and Kelly offer an initial summary of core values as follows:

- valuing and respecting all individuals, groups and communities – their work, their abilities, their rights, their contributions to society and their cultural resources;
- valuing oneself;
- autonomy of individuals and groups;
- justice and equality;
- the right to participate in decisions and actions where one is a stakeholder;
- moral accountability towards those affected by one's actions;
- the obligation to monitor and regularly review one's own behaviour, practice and relationships;
- lifelong learning and development for all.

They then go on to suggest seven core areas in which competences in youth and community work might be defined:

1 self-awareness, self-management, self-evaluation and self-development;
2 establishing relationships of trust with individuals, groups and communities;
3 involving groups and communities in participative approaches to learning;
4 working with individuals to promote personal and social development;
5 working in teams for organisations and in association with other agencies;

6 planning and evaluation in consultation with stakeholders;
7 organisation and management of people and resources (Erault and Kelly, 1994).

This account builds on a number of statements of the core skills involved in community work and youth work and is broadly connected to similar processes of definition taking place in community care and in counselling and psychotherapy. Erault and Kelly claim to have consulted these discussions in other disciplines when drawing up the statement for youth and community work.

Of course, there is a continuing debate about the definition of practice as an accumulation of skills. However, it is important to notice that it is on this basis that a good deal of agreement has been reached about the role of youth and community workers.

The work of informal education

From being perceived as glorified caretakers of buildings or as 'soft cops' with the gift of 'keeping young people off the streets' and quelling riot, the specific educational style and focus of youth and community work has become sought after by other professionals in the 1990s. The potential contribution of youth workers and community workers has been recognised in the context of the changes in welfare and schooling brought about by the Thatcher administration. For example, the role of teachers has become much more tightly defined in terms of the National Curriculum, and yet, at the same time, schools are to be held much more closely responsible for aspects of the social life of pupils. Schools will be publicly accountable for their record on school attendance, for example. These contradictory demands leave teachers in a highly contradictory role, and the skills of youth and community workers are particularly valued at this point because they attend to aspects of the social education curriculum and to educational processes which have been squeezed to the margins of schooling.

In the context of Conservative reforms of education, there has been enormous pressure to redefine the skills of educators as skills in the management and delivery of services. Much of the impetus to define the role and analyse the skills of youth and community workers has come from professional associations and trade unions. Such bodies have been keen to value the group work, networking and work with individuals undertaken by their members, rather than allow this work to be undervalued in comparison to the equally necessary work of fundraising, budgeting, staff appointment, team-building, report-writing, project evaluation, staff appraisal, and so on.

Feminist practice has something to contribute to all of these debates and discussions. The aim here is to show how some of the terms that have come to form a 'professional common sense' can be criticised and extended from within feminist debate, and how insights from feminist practice can be useful to the whole profession.

The resources of the woman educator

A woman educator always works at a number of boundaries. She draws on her personal resources enormously. Many women youth and community workers, when asked where they derive their strength to continue with the work, make reference to their friends and families, particularly their mothers and their children, as a source of love, strength and support. Women educators also draw on their political analysis of the position of girls and women within the communities they are working with. Here she may draw on a history of involvement with campaigns, on reading and study, and on shared reflection with others, inside and outside the profession, with whom she can make common cause. She may also draw on a professional network of resources, including opportunities for staff development, for training and for supervision of her practice. In all her interventions, personal, political and professional elements are drawn on. Each may contribute to her success or difficulty in undertaking the work.

Some existing accounts do stress the part played by the personality and character of the worker in the success of their work. One very attractive account by Fred Milson does this. Milson was already arguing in 1970 that: 'In the matter of personal qualities, one wonders if the pendulum has not swung too far in the direction of a detached and "professional" attitude' (Milson, 1970, p.78). He goes on to say:

> The successful operator uses rather than suppresses his personality whilst checking any tendency to be subjective in his judgements or to be un- consciously satisfying of his own needs rather than the needs of young people in his efforts. (Milson, 1970, p.78)

He identifies three qualities found to be rewarding for the processes of social education: (1) imagination, linked to 'that undiscourageable faith in people's possibilities which is the mark of the true educator'; (2) the ability to work as a member of a team, and (3) 'the ability to grow as people with the work we are doing' (Milson, 1970, pp.78–9). The authors of *The Management of Detached Work* suggest that an appropriate match between the worker's personality and the nature of the project is a key both to success in detached work and some of the characteristic difficulties of managing it (Arnold et al., 1981).

Most recent writing sets out a professional code of practice with an explicit set of professional values. Such writing is usually relatively depersonalised. It also makes little reference to its own historical context. It is almost as if all the developments in community-based work with young people were leading up to this point of professional clarity, from which there can now be little movement. So, Mark Smith, whose excellent accounts of informal and local education have done much to establish a consensus about the profession, suggested that the key question to be asked of any youth work interventions is 'Does it facilitate learning?' (Smith, 1988). And the major question to be asked by interviewers focusing on a task-based and skills-based approach to practice are: 'Does this person show evidence of possessing the appropriate knowledge, skills and values to perform the work that has been identified?'

There have also been occasional attempts to develop definitions of the worker's role in which a social/political or theological/religious analysis offers the guiding framework for intervention. These can take both a conservative and a progressive form. The goals of practice are then both highly specific and of global and transhistorical importance: 'to do my duty to God and the queen', 'Black community development', 'liberation', 'socialist character-building' (see, for example, Chauhan, 1989; Taylor, 1987).

The distinctiveness of feminist practice

Given that approaches to practice have either emphasised the personality of the worker or the professional code or the political goals of the work, the distinctiveness of feminist-inspired practice lies in an ability and desire to connect these aspects of the work and to draw on them critically. Such practice can look to a whole body of thinking, professional work, political practice and personal transformation that grew from the slogan 'The personal is political.' So, feminist workers would reject the commonly-held view that there are people who show 'natural gifts' as educators – and would, for example, recognise that being 'naturally a good listener' (in the case of a woman) or a 'natural leader' (in the case of a man) is a profoundly social creation of the gender system. Yet, like Fred Milson, a feminist perspective would place a strong emphasis on the person. 'Professional skills' and 'political analysis' cannot be detached from the person of the worker. Unlike Fred Milson (at least as he was writing in 1970), feminists know that persons can be women.

There is an important sense of *being* as well as *doing* in feminist practice. Who a woman is, as well as how she acts, the whole history, conscious and unconscious, of how she has become a woman: this all matters in the form of education she can offer. This is not to claim that identity is the sole source of good practice in education, and certainly not to claim that shared identity is the basis of good practice. However, it does mean that she actively consults her own sense of her self and her own agenda in any work she undertakes. For example, becoming a mother clearly changes the way women workers work with young women's groups. Black women may decide their resources are best used in working with other Black women and building coalitions across different Black communities. A worker who is questioning her own sexuality may decide not to work on issues about sexuality with a group at that point. Or it may seem the right moment to do so. There is no formula for 'the conscious use of self in relation to others', but it is this history and archaeology of the self on which our practice draws. In this, feminist educators draw on a humanist tradition of ethics, with a stress on an attention to particular people in particular moments, rather than on precepts or maxims as a substitute for this attention.

So, one of the characteristics of feminist practice is the way a woman worker can draw on her own resources as a person, and is supported to do that, within the context of a professional code, and always with the aim of extending the learning and development of the young women as her priority. There has been a great emphasis on the importance of supervision as a place where the links with the personal can be explored. This leads to a re-integration of the personal within the context of professional/political discussions. It means that her own learning and development is not counterposed to the learning of the young women she is working with. As Fred Milson remarked, youth work provides a fine liberal education. At the same time, the issue of developing appropriate professional boundaries is of the utmost importance. It is important, although difficult, both to acknowledge the mutuality of the learning process and to maintain a distinction from friendship.

This theme of connection in learning can be explored further in relation to the following key terms of professional common sense:

- experiential learning;
- problem-posing /problem-solving;
- participation and group work;
- advocacy;
- development.

Experiential learning

It is often claimed that the tradition of learning from experience has its roots in the writings of the American pragmatists, and in particular in the work of John Dewey. 'Experiential learning' also refers to a process of social learning not contained in the formal elements of the National Curriculum for schools in England and Wales. It has also been given such names as 'the school of hard knocks' and 'the university of life'. In youth and community work, 'experiential learning' usually refers to 'learning by doing' rather than 'learning by instruction'. Sometimes it means the opportunity to take part in new activities and experiences, to 'broaden the horizons'. Sometimes, the project of experiential learning can offer support for 'going to the roots': reflection on the difficult and positive experiences of life within a particular group/community. Knowledge and understanding are believed to be the results of such learning processes, rather than to arise as a result of instruction. It is an educational tradition capable of inspiring passionate adherence. And yet the concept of 'experience' on which it is based is one of the most slippery in the whole of philosophy, and because of the difficulties associated with it, 'experience' has often been rejected altogether as a useful term.

However, the sense that traditional models of learning erase the experience and knowledge of subordinated groups remains acute, despite numerous philosophical critiques of the concept of 'experience'. The claims of 'experience' as a touchstone against which social and political strategies for emancipation can be tested remain vital. There can surely be no political emancipation of women without an engagement with the day-to-day realities and experiences of many different groups of women. And, although experience cannot speak itself without language, language has to be scrutinised for its ability to communicate and express, or to disguise, the things that matter in relation to the lived realities of particular groups of women.

It is interesting that even in universities, feminist teachers have reflected in depth on the place of 'experience' in the development of women's studies. Donna Haraway (1991) argues that experience still continues to be central to women's studies. She emphasises, however, that it is reflection on experience, the process of making sense of experience which constitutes the explosive terrain of political change, rather than 'experience' alone. Haraway writes:

> Women do not find 'experience' ready to hand any more than they/we find 'nature' or 'the body' preformed always innocent and waiting outside the violations of language and culture. Just as nature is one of culture's most startling and non-innocent products, so is experience one of the least innocent, least self-evident aspects of historical, embodied movement. Through the politically explosive terrain of linked experience, feminists make connection and enter into movement. Complexity, heterogeneity, specific positioning and power-charged difference are not the same thing as liberal pluralism. Experience is a semiosis, an embodying of meanings ... The politics of difference that feminists need to articulate must be rooted in a politics of experience that searches for specificity, heterogeneity, and connection through struggle, not through psychologistic, liberal appeals to each her own endless difference. Feminism is collective; and difference is political, that is about power, accountability and hope. Experience, like difference, is about contradictory and necessary connection. (Haraway, 1991, p.109)

Making sense of experience is making meanings of struggle and connection

This hopeful account of the place of learning from experience as a place of learning from struggle and connection can be of enormous benefit to youth and community workers, and it points to the role of the educator in assisting young women in making sense of existing and new experiences. When young women make sense of experience and make connections between aspects of their lives and the lives of other women which they had previously held separate, they are acting as feminist theorists as much as anyone involved in academic work as a trade.

Here, briefly, are two examples of the kind of 'making sense' process which is being discussed here.

The mothers and daughters project, Cheetham Hill

A group of young women attending the club were having difficulties with their parents, who didn't want them to be out at night. One of the workers was a mother of daughters herself and felt that she could understand the parents' anxieties. Some of the mothers were members of a community group which met at the community centre during the day.

The worker decided to set up a 'mothers and daughters' project, to enable each group to express their own perspective. The young women experienced their mothers as lacking in trust. The mothers were fearful that their daughters would 'get in trouble'. The fear of trouble was sexual, but not only sexual.

The method the workers chose as a starting point for the work was, firstly, to undertake in-depth interviews with both mothers and daughters, and then to develop a life-history project. In this storytelling project, the girls became the chroniclers and the storytellers of their mothers' lives. Beautiful, bound biographies were produced, with photographs and narratives.

The worker's aim of establishing trust once more was certainly achieved, and across the truly explosive terrain of mother–daughter differences, some new understandings of women's condition of life in a North Manchester community were generated.

Using photography

Photography has been used in a number of projects as a basis for reflection on experience and struggle over meanings. Feminist work in cultural studies has created an understanding of the power of visual images in shaping women's experience, self-understanding and subordination/

survival. Informal education projects working with young women are able to explore the impact of visual images, often through young women becoming creators of their own images. The following focuses of work have been extremely popular.

Critical reflection on magazines, especially on advertising

Here workers use collage work, ideas about 'positive' and 'negative' images, focus on representations of 'body parts' in relation to discussions of ideas about beauty and female sexuality

Photography and video workshops

Young women produce their own alternative posters, photo-stories and videos. As well as giving access to the idea that images are 'productions' as well as 'representations', projects of this kind have given young women a forum in which to discuss relationships, romance and their own dreams and fantasies. Using photo-collage to develop young women's fantasies has been a successful method. Here, young women use photographs of themselves and then amend or combine them in order to produce dream images and alternative scenes. Photography combines with crayon, Tipp-Ex and felt-tip pen as the raw material of dreams and fantasies. The photo-love/alternative endings storyline has also been very popular. Common alternative endings to the 'girl gets together with boy' storyline are: girls successfully resisting rape, and girls dumping their boyfriends in order to stick with their best friends.

Photography is also very powerful for the exploration of anti-racist and international perspectives. Visual images are very important in the construction of Black women's identities in Britain and globally. There is still an absence of representation of European Black women, with North American imagery being the dominant source of representations. Women from the southern hemisphere are usually depicted as impoverished, backward, victims, grateful recipients of aid. Or else they are represented as entirely 'other' and as the repositories of a smouldering sensuality available for the dominant North to consume.

Development education projects have used images from the South to challenge such dominant representations. The practice in one development education project was to fund photographers to work with poor communities over a period of time in both Somalia and Pakistan to produce more appropriate images. Rehana Hussain, a youth and community worker working with women from Asian communities in Sheffield, recognised the power of such images for her own practice in building and retaining community links. However, she also pointed out that the reception of such images, even among communities now settled here but with strong connections with the South, needed attention and work. The worker has a vital role to play in assisting in the interpretation of such images and the creation of meanings which challenge the codes of 'otherness' (Hussain, 1994).

Learning by problem-posing and problem-solving: Think opportunity, not problem

The movement from being pathologised as a source of problems to being able to recognise the dynamic between the fact that limitations are being placed on us and our own possibly self-destructive response to these limitations is an educational movement and a liberating one. When so many official discourses problematise young women, it is good to be able to turn the tables and to point to official discourses and practices as often themselves the source of the problem.

The Activate Group

> The Activate Group is a mixed group of black and white young women. Initially, due to the difficulties they were having at school, we enabled them to explore these difficulties and ideas for action. This involved them coming up with proposals for changes (concerning racism, sexism and respect from teachers) they would like to see in school; choosing teachers they felt would listen; arranging a series of meetings with them on their territory to discuss these proposals. Some positive outcomes arose due to the teachers listening to them and taking on board some of their suggestions and involving some of the young women in their implementation. (Terry et al., 1993, p.19)

This brief account of the work of a Leeds-based group gives a clear indication of the critical role of problem-posing and problem-solving as a method. It involves a clear shift away from seeing girls as a problem or as basically having to learn to become women who deal with other people's problems. The motto of the Leeds young women's workers is 'Think opportunity, not problem'. Young women themselves define the starting points and terms for the work. To begin with, workers might identify, from discussions with young women, key areas that are influencing their lives. Through group discussion, workers might begin to identify the voices and perspectives that influence young women's thinking about the chosen topic. There are a number of useful methods here: discussion of newspaper reports, current episodes in soap operas, magazine features, especially problem pages, drama exercises and focusing on popular music all provide resources. The second stage is a process of positive identification of starting points by young women and the workers themselves.

'Youth' has long been seen as a problem, and the terms from which 'the problem of youth' is constructed – such as unemployment, crime and deviance, the transition to adult status – are focused for young women through attention to sexuality. Youth and community work practice can clearly contribute to the pathologising of young women. Consciousness-raising about these powerful definitions of young women's experience is always an important starting point. It can seem as if to be young means constantly to be measuring yourself against a standard of 'normality' and finding yourself lacking. Conversations about what is 'normal' and who decides, if continued over time and offered in a context of positive opportunities, can help young women shake off some of the effects of negative ascriptions as 'deviant' or 'a problem'.

Avoiding contributing to mistaken pathologising

Youth and community work practice needs to avoid adding to the pathologising of young women. For example, community and youth work practice has often focused on the assessment of needs. This potentially places young women in a position of passivity, waiting to have their needs met by others.

While recognising the power of the language of basic needs to enable women to make some call on resources, the language of rights should also be used, as this encapsulates women's participation as citizens in defining and seeking solutions for social problems. A good example of this process of working on the definition of problems and needs is in the common process of working with young women with small children. Quite often, the attention of young women focuses initially on the problem of what to do with the children and on the needs of the children for play facilities. A youth and community worker's involvement in establishing a mother and toddler group may also assist the process of young women exploring their own needs, as mothers, for time away from the children. It may even eventually lead to a questioning of what is expected of mothers in our society, and to discussion of the rights of women *vis-à-vis* the rights of men.

Learning through participation and group work

Feminist practice attempts to develop ways of working which move away from hierarchy and towards democratic organisation. It also attempts to move away from individual pathologising and blaming, towards a participation in community groups and networks, a sense of citizenship and the right to influence the direction of society.

There is a growing literature on group work as a key method in community action and in feminist education. bell hooks, the Black feminist educator and cultural critic, writes:

> Small groups remain an important place for education for critical consciousness for a number of reasons. An especially important aspect of the small group setting is the emphasis on communicating feminist thinking, feminist theory in a manner that can easily be understood. In small groups, individuals do not need to be equally literate or literate at all because the information is primarily shared through conversation, through dialogue which is necessarily a liberatory expression. (Literacy should be a goal for feminists even as we ensure it is not a requirement for participation in feminist education.) Reforming small groups would subvert the appropriation of feminist thinking by a select group of academic women and men, usually white, from privileged class backgrounds. (hooks, 1989, p.24)

Understanding of the place of small groups as a vehicle for education has developed in tension with therapeutic accounts of group work. The educational focus of group work demands that connections be made between the work of the group and life outside the group. Therapeutic accounts more often draw on group processes themselves as a source of healing.

Group work can be undertaken informally. It can also be undertaken within an explicit and agreed framework, with links to the curriculum of formal education. The worker characteristically develops programmes of work, study, community action and social events in discussion and negotiation with young women whom she has come to know, often using already existing friendship networks as a basis for building up a project.

It is at this early stage that many choices are made about the focus and membership of groups, and it is also here that exclusions occur. Sometimes, it is only later that these patterns of exclusion are noticed and addressed. For example, a worker working in a 'racially mixed' neighbourhood notices recruits from only one group in the neighbourhood: the one to which she is most closely connected herself. At an early stage in its work, Hulme Girls' Project in Manchester, which was established in the same building as the oldest Lads' Club in the area, addressed this issue and began a programme of positive work with Black girls. Here, the worker describes building up and working with a group of 14 young Black mothers:

> Since the very encouraging beginning, we have built up our experience and a more ambitious plan of activity. This was based on what we felt was now possible with this group and on what the young women have said was needed, this includes:

1 Courses on woodwork, basic electrics, computers.
2 Discussion using Open University work packs on women and health issues and other relevant topics.
3 Support work with young women before they leave school at our local school, using informal contacts and home visits, also special sessions.
4 Preparation and build-up for the Educational Exchange Visit to Jamaica, including:
  Educational courses on Jamaica – January to March.
  Preparation – history, culture, Black women in history, women's issues, historical buildings and places in Jamaica.

We feel that the work has developed in a way that really holds together and involves the group members as it is highly relevant to them and their lives. (Hulme Girls' Project, 1984, p.4)

The aim of such a programme is clearly to develop the understandings of the group. The worker's ability to respond to the issues and potentials introduced by group members is critical. It is the worker's interest in the agendas of young women which is often the catalyst which allows young women to move from being consumers to creators, from being cast in a role of dependency to one of active participation.

The other aspect of such community-based group work which cannot be stressed too strongly is the necessity of continual outreach work and of workers getting to know individuals well in their own right, before and during the time they are members of a group. It is on the basis of such knowledge of individuals and the building up of relationships of trust that workers can feel free sometimes to jettison programmes and arranged agendas in favour of responding to issues in the here and now:

Last night one of the young women brought her new baby into the club with her. We jettisoned the planned talk on drugs which I had carefully prepared and we talked for hours in the girls' room about having babies or not and relationships. The fact that Jane was there with her baby and was talking seriously made the young women listen to her and join in in a way they would never have listened to me. (Moore, 1994, p.5)

This comment came from a student on placement, working with a girls' group in a youth club. It beautifully encapsulates what is involved, both in the effort to plan learning through small group work, and even more importantly, in the ability to let those plans go.

Working with small groups is the central focus and defining feature of informal education practice. Group work forms the crucible from which other ways of working emerge:

- working with individuals in the role of counsellor and advocate;
- working with groups to promote mutual aid, linked to collective action and campaigning.

Learning through advocacy

Information as a resource

The youth and community worker has been memorably described as 'useful friend'. The usefulness lies, above all, in access to information. Information is power.

Working with girls requires the worker to become a walking resource centre, equipped with up-to-date knowledge on money, housing, health and maternity rights. A number of projects have concentrated initially on building up an information resource and have focused a good deal of attention on understanding young women's rights, both to resources and to participation in processes that affect their lives. Information packs are constructed with the assistance and participation of young women in the project. They characteristically include information about benefits and health services for women, information about other resources for young people and women's groups in the borough and surrounding area, information about Women's Aid and Rape Crisis, information about Lesbian Link and groups for young lesbians/young bisexual women. They may also include information about concessionary travel and other cheap or free services, including leisure facilities. They may include information relating to homelessness, including matters such as where to find free cleaning and laundry facilities. They will direct workers and young women to other specialist advice projects, such as Citizens' Advice Bureaux and law centres. Some projects have specific information and experience in relation to industrial tribunals, particularly where there is a claim of race or sex discrimination.

However, the availability of such information is only part of the story. Hence the importance of the term 'friend' in the expression 'useful friend.' It is the friendliness, accessibility, reliability and dependability of the relationship a worker has with young women which can make information accessible. But the term 'friend' may disguise at least as much as it reveals. The relationship between a woman worker and the young women she works with is certainly based on mutuality. However, it is not based on equality in the way of friendship.

Codes of ethics

It is important to recognise some of the difficulties involved in offering friendship on a professional basis, and there are a number of important questions about professional boundaries that have developed here. Lesbian workers, in particular, have been instrumental in developing codes of ethics which can assist in recognising when you are becoming over-involved, while also recognising the dangers of apparently detached professionalism. Receiving payment to undertake the work of informal education, or even undertaking such work in a voluntary capacity, does place serious limits and responsibilities on workers, which women, on the whole, have been quick to recognise. Codes of ethics have been developed which include statements about:

- non-violence and non-discrimination;
- health and safety of women workers;
- the importance of co-working;
- use of project funds to buy items for young people, particularly payment for alcohol and cigarettes;
- the non-permissibility of sexual relationships;
- the importance of reliability in relationships with young women;
- the importance of reliability in timekeeping;
- how crisis situations will be dealt with;
- availability of workers' home telephone numbers;
- confidentiality and the limits of confidentiality.

The benefits of such a clear statement lie in allowing the boundaries of the work to be made explicit, shared and discussed. It means that young women know that while a worker may become very involved with their lives and be a very important source of support and advocacy in the context of power systems which they are forced to deal with, the relationship is a professional one, in which the young woman has certain rights and the worker has some very clear responsibilities. The relationship does not impose on the young women personal obligations to provide support to the worker, and although the worker always learns a great deal from her work, the relationship does not have the purpose of enabling the worker to explore her own difficulties.

Collective advocacy

Advocacy work need not be limited to work with individuals, and the process of collective self-advocacy has strong links with concepts of community development. Work with groups, which may begin as self-help or mutual aid, often has implications for women beyond the ambit of those small groups, and feminist practice must encourage the making of connections, especially with the people and agencies which have the power to create positive change.

The Y-Wait Group in North Manchester Health Authority offers an important model of young women's participation in a self-help project which has had a significant impact on the power structures of the health authority.

The group began as an initiative of young women in a community centre in a North Manchester estate, who felt that the services their GPs offered were not appropriate to young women of the area. They established their own group with the support of a community health worker, employed their own nurse and began to develop projects which could reach out to young women in the area, for whom the current services seemed out of reach and inappropriate. There was a strong emphasis on sexual health in the project, and the group became seen as a pioneer of 'peer education' within the health authority, facilitating a determined rethinking of the health authority's own approach and publicity.

Learning through development

The critical role of group work in promoting learning means that the worker has a responsibility both to support individuals who participate in their programmes and towards community groups whose interests are wider and more generalised than those of the particular small groups she is involved with. In responding to the first responsibility, she may find herself concerned with the themes of personal development. In responding to the second, wider responsibility, she will find herself concerned with themes of community development.

There are a number of difficulties associated with the term 'development' which it is important to highlight at this point. These have been analysed in relation to child development by Erica Burman (1994) and in relation to economic development by Maria Mies and Vandana Shiva (1993). Like the term 'community', the term 'development' is capable of imparting a warm glow while bearing a number of different meanings.

Youth workers need to recognise the highly-normative connotations of the term in the context of both personal and economic development. There are highly-elaborated accounts of stages of growth (often rooted in biology) to which all individuals and societies are expected to conform. These models of 'normal development' which claim universal validity are masculinist and rooted in Western capitalist power, relying on a concept of progress which appears to see the experience of North American societies and of successful young men in such societies as the goal of development.

It is therefore essential that women workers are aware of the normative pressures contained in the term 'development', which may, for example, be used by other professionals, such as educational psychologists, or by funding bodies concerned with urban regeneration. They can then frame their own projects and ways of working to permit young women (and themselves) some say in what constitutes progress and development for them, some control over the agenda of 'development projects'.

In community development work, this often involves extensive and carefully thought-through consultation processes and the creation of non-bureaucratic democratic forums. In the context of unequal and unjust social relations, this is likely to lead to conflict over priorities with funding and resourcing bodies, and women need to have strategies for engaging in or avoiding such conflict. For example, in relation to personal development, 'normal development' for a young woman is understood as progress to heterosexuality. There is therefore a positive need to validate lesbian relationships. This is likely to be in conflict with funding bodies' agenda of promoting good contraceptive knowledge to girls and young women.

In relation to community development, there is an apparently permanent economic conflict between a self-help agenda which believes the costs of welfare can be reduced by community development and the clear demands of most community-based groups for more resources, and in particular for more sustained opportunities for employment.

Young women's centres as a focus for personal development and community development

Wigan Youth Service developed a number of young women's centres during the 1980s, and these offered a focus both for personal development and community development. Worsley Mesnes Young Women's Centre pioneered an approach to work with young women based on young women's rights, which linked advocacy, personal development and community development. The following extracts from one project report illustrates some of the methods which the workers used:

> Following a supervision session, it was decided to do some work on the rights and entitlements of young women particularly looking at young women's rights in terms of:
>
> 1 The individual
> 2 The project
> 3 The local community
> 4 Wider social and political issues.

The workers then chose a number of themes to address. Under the heading 'The Right to Live Free From Abuse: Physical, Sexual, Emotional', they considered the following matters:

T034198

1   The individual
   - Information – refuges, rape crisis, solicitors.
   - Space for one-to-one work.
   - Self-esteem and confidence.
   - Don't judge young women who stay in violent relationships.
   - Support and training for workers.
   - Links with other agencies.
2   The project
   - Make sure information is available, put in the toilet (private) and kitchen (public).
   - We create an environment that refuses to accept that abuse is OK.
   - Create physical space for one-to-one work.
   - Keep all project members informed and updated.
   - Make the ethos of the project groups safe for young women to talk about violence.
3   The community
   - Housing Department – policy on rehousing women poor but good relationships with local housing officer ensure it happens.
   - Work with young men: issues for estate worker team.
   - Ensure new workers from other departments understand our perspective on this issue.
   - Links with other women on estate through meetings etc. means project is an educational force on this issue.
4   Wider social and political issues
   - Wigan Youth Service Homelessness Group – liaison with Housing and CHAR to seek changes in policy on young women's housing.
   - No rape crisis in Wigan or support groups.
   - Contribute to development of guidelines on sexual abuse and to training programmes for professionals.
   - Campaigning against violence against women.
   - Refuge in Wigan not linked to Women's Aid.
   - Issue of rape in marriage.
   - Treatment of women in rape trials.
   - Make links nationally with bodies doing work on these issues.

Having made their current thinking in each of these areas explicit, the workers then identified an action plan of work which they could tackle.

Making voices heard: The basic necessity of literacy as an aspect and method of practice

The themes from professional common sense – experiential learning, learning through problem-posing and problem-solving, learning through group work and participation, learning through advocacy and learning through development – can all be understood as moments in a process of education for liberation. The writer who most crystallised these processes for educators of recent generations is Paolo Freire. In order to contribute to a project of empowerment or liberation, all these processes are to be rooted in an explicit commitment to literacy. Not to a merely functional literacy either, but to a literacy whose purpose is to enable those who are denied expression and participation in the current social order to act in ways which transform their own condition.

Although Freire's (1972) work on the nature of consciousness and authenticity and the relation between consciousness, education and liberation has been developed and modified, its central themes remain of the utmost importance. It is, after all, still the oppression/liberation axis which remains the focus of attention in feminist work with girls and young women. The complexity and heterogeneity of the experience of oppression and the project of liberation is now widely recognised. The poet June Jordan expressed this brilliantly in her essay, 'Report from the Bahamas':

> When we get the monsters off our backs, we may all want to run in very different directions. (Jordan, 1989, p.144)

In this essay, June Jordan is exploring the basis for alliances against a shared oppression which recognise a diversity of visions of liberation:

> I am reaching for the words to describe the difference between a common identity that has been imposed and the individual identity any one of us will choose, once she gains that chance ... I am saying that the ultimate connection cannot be the enemy. The ultimate connection must be the need that we find between us. It is not only who you are, in other words, but what we can do for each other, that will determine the connection. (Jordan, 1989, p.144)

Such a recognition of the need for alliance to be constructed across diversities, rather than recognised, once we are in the process of release from a state of alienation, modifies some central aspects of Freire's account. In creating opportunities for young women to 'name their own monsters' and to speak about their visions of the future, youth and community workers quickly discover that young women all want to run in different directions. The movement of feminist work is away from an imposed common identity as 'women' to a place where we choose our own connectedness of mutual support, and solidarity is not an automatic effect of consciousness-raising. Education programmes must actively and consciously promote this. Freire's emphasis on voice, language and literacy and his claim that 'silence' remains the single great theme of emancipatory education will be recognised by feminist educators very clearly.

The movement from silence to speech is of central importance to many aspects of the role of the woman worker. In all the case studies which have been used in this chapter, it is this moment of finding and giving voice which is critical. It may be daughters giving voice to their understandings of their mothers; it may be a young women's group giving voice to a sense of the importance of their history as Black women, or young women writing a photo-love story with a different kind of ending and giving voice to hopes differing from the hopes of heterosexual romance. It may be young women asserting their rights not to be discriminated against. It may be young women asserting their needs for health care to be offered in appropriate and non-patronising ways. It may be young women collectively voicing the need for resources: whether of housing or of play facilities or of free education. All these processes are underpinned by literacy as a basic necessity, and all participate clearly in that movement from silence to speech, from object to subject, which Freire identified as the basic movement of education for liberation.

5 Sexuality

Friends

You hold my hand
Smile and talk
We're friends aren't we
Would you walk off
Or hold me close
I want to hold you
    Kiss you
You let go of my hand
    Hug me
And turn to leave
I call your name
    You turn
    I smile
Maybe I'll tell you tomorrow
(Shona, Manchester Young Lesbian Group, 1992, p.6)

Talking about sex and sexuality is inescapable in talking about girls and young women. The poem above expresses clearly some of the uncertainties involved in the expression of sexuality for young women, the fears of rejection and the links between love and friendship, between affection and sex, which are so important in one common experience of female sexuality. The poem could plausibly have been written about a possible boyfriend. In fact, it was written by a member of Manchester Young Lesbian Group and is about another girl.

Sex and sexuality are widely understood to be defining preoccupations of adolescence. Women pass from girlhood to womanhood in ways which are understood as essentially to do with female sexuality. Some feminist theorists have suggested that sexuality is the main mechanism of female subordination: 'Sexuality is to feminism what work is to marxism: that which is most one's own , yet most taken away' (MacKinnon, 1982, p.1). It is not necessary to share this view to understand that this is important ground for informal education with girls and young women.

Yet the question of what is understood by sexuality and its link to sexual practice remains oddly obscure. Women workers are used to having their sexuality questioned. It is sometimes assumed that we must all be queer, simply because we choose to do separate and autonomous work with girls. For many people, sexuality seems to be linked to a taken-for-granted sense of self-identity. In our society, it is linked to gender. In order to grow up heterosexual, one must identify as a woman or as a man. A woman who does not identify as heterosexual throws the dominant understandings of gender – what it means to be a proper woman or a proper man – into confusion. To gain a positive lesbian or bisexual identity, young women are forced to question such dominant understandings of gender, and in particular to question the norms of femininity they are offered. When young women undertake such questioning, they share common ground with a feminist project which identifies and tries to change the restrictive patterns associated with conventional, dominant models of femininity.

Our understanding of our sexuality is clearly linked to our sexual desires and our actual or anticipated choices about sexual practice. Sexuality encompasses far more than sexual practice and should not be reduced to it. At the same time, it is impossible to speak and write about sexuality without speaking and writing about sex.

There has been an important recognition, arising in the context of AIDS/HIV education, but building on much earlier work, that girls need the chance to learn about their bodies and to talk about sex. Many women workers have found material produced in the AIDS/HIV education world, particularly the AVERT materials, useful (Aggleton et al., 1990). Education about sexuality and education about sex are separate and connected areas of work. This chapter aims to offer a series of approaches and methods to work on both sexuality and sexual practice, from both heterosexual and lesbian perspectives.

What is sexuality? Current frameworks

First, it is useful to consider some of the available frameworks for understanding sexuality, which can be shared with young women in the context of informal education.

Sexology and developmental psychology

Probably the most widely available account of human sexuality is still the one which derives from sexology. The successful achievement of heterosexual identity at adolescence is seen as a key developmental task. For a woman, this also involves a recognition that her satisfactory, normal, heterosexual development is bound up with the possibility of becoming a mother. The precarious path to the achievement of this prized, normative identity is littered with difficulties and distractions, including the fact that even according to the sexologists, 'exclusive heterosexuality' is only one end of a continuum of possible orientations. For example, Kinsey, whose surveys of sexual behaviour have offered a continuingly influential framework to link sexuality with sexual practice, used a 0–6 scale to rate individual's sexual orientation:

0   exclusively heterosexual;
1   predominantly heterosexual, only incidental homosexuality;
2   predominantly heterosexual, but more than incidentally homosexual;
3   equally heterosexual and homosexual;
4   predominantly homosexual, but more than incidentally heterosexual;
5   predominantly homosexual, but only incidentally heterosexual;
6   exclusively homosexual. (Kinsey, 1948)

The variety of human experience of our sexualities has been mapped by the sexologists onto a continuum with 'same' at one end and 'different' at the other. This continuum does not appear to be gendered. Along the way to 'normal' heterosexual relations, many of us are understood, even by sexologists, to enter into the 'passing phase' of same-sex friendships and homo-erotic relationships. The dominant available model regards such same-sex relationships, at best, as a mark of immaturity and, at worst, as sickness or perversion. It is here that the feminist critiques begin. For, if it so 'normal' and 'natural' to pass through the phase of same-sex attractions, why does 'growing up normal' need so much encouragement and attention? From this point of view, accounts of adolescent development which assume that heterosexuality is normative fail to account either for growing up gay or growing up straight.

There are now writers who retain a psychosexual model of development but who are more positive about gay identity. They tend to separate the developmental task of achieving a strong identity at adolescence from the presumption that this identity must be heterosexual. Achieving a strong identity is argued to be a developmental task to be accomplished as an adolescent. It is possible to achieve such a sense of identity as a homosexual. It is possible to be normal and well-adjusted and gay.

However, for feminists, the developmental psychology models have long appeared problematic. They are highly normative, and the account they give of 'developmental tasks', whether for heterosexuals or homosexuals, is strongly masculinised. Motherhood appears as the pinnacle of female sexuality.

Psycho-analysis

Despite the fact that the traditions of psycho-analysis have offered a profoundly denigratory account of femininity, feminists have sometimes found the engagement with and critique of psycho-analytic accounts of female desire more attractive than the models of developmental psychology. Perhaps this is because they offer an attention to the meanings of desires, and do not simply concentrate on behaviours. In drawing our attention to meanings, such accounts hold open the possibilities of change of interpretation:

> The psycho-analytic concept of sexuality ... can never be equated with genitality nor is it the simple expression of a biological drive. It is always psycho-sexuality, a system of conscious and unconscious human fantasies involving a range of excitations and activities that produce pleasure beyond the satisfaction of any physiological need. It arises from various sources, seeks satisfaction in many different ways and makes use of many diverse objects for its aim of achieving pleasure. (Mitchell and Rose, 1982, p.2)

Our sexuality is always, in this perspective, about our pleasures and desires and the meanings we give to them, rather than primarily about our behaviours, although psycho-analytic accounts do acknowledge the ways in which these desires shape our behaviours. Feminist accounts attempt to change dominant understanding of female sexuality and female desire. I have identified three different feminist perspectives which can inform practice.

Sexuality as a social construction

In this approach, a great deal of attention is paid to the ways in which female sexuality is constructed through social practices which tend towards the production of a preferred, if not compulsory, heterosexuality for girls and women:

> Young women are under pressure to construct their material bodies into a particular model of femininity which is both inscribed on the surface of their bodies, through such skills as dress, make up and dietary regimes, and disembodied in the sense of detachment from their sensuality and alienation from their material bodies. (Holland et al., 1994. p.24)

This 'particular model of femininity' is a model of heterosexuality, but its forms are very particularly created and change for each generation of young women. Close attention to dress and appearance, including attention to body weight and shape, have been preoccupations of femininity since the mass-circulation women's magazines of the nineteenth century made them so (Beetham, 1996).

The 'teenage market' is a market for the commodities of femininity: clothes, hair accessories, diet products, exercise videos, make-up. It is also a market for the changing icons of femininity and heterosexuality in popular culture: the teenage magazines promote the heroes of pop music, the stars of the soaps, the narratives of romance and, increasingly, the moralities and techniques of sexual intercourse as sources of instruction in femininity and heterosexuality. The social construction of sexuality occurs in part through the purchase and consumption of particular commodities, including a consumption of their meanings.

These constructions of femininity have always had strong class connotations too, with different magazines promoting different products, depending on the purchasing power of their readers. They also produce a clear identification of femininity with 'fairness' in skin colour, constructing all Black women as deviant by definition. The sexuality of Black women has, then, largely been understood in relation to this White 'norm'.

It can also be argued that the pleasure and desire associated with sexuality by the psycho-analytic tradition is caught up with this process of buying and using commodities, making the work of producing a successful heterosexual identity a potentially highly-desirable and highly-pleasurable process.

Interactions between boys and girls, men and women in small groups and in organisations, such as schools and youth projects, can also be understood as integral not only to the formation of gender identity, but also to the formation of heterosexuality. There are now a number of classroom studies which demonstrate the nature of sexist behaviour and sexual harassment in classrooms, including the use of sexually explicit and derogatory language to control girls and to maintain boys' dominance (Herbert, 1992; Jones and Mahoney, 1989). This work reflects on the question of activity and passivity in sexuality. Is female sexuality constructed as passive in relation to the activity of the male? Do girls still have to wait to be asked and take what they are offered? Can we recognise women's own active participation in the constructions of our sexuality?

This theme of women's active participation in the construction of female heterosexuality as passive is an important one for the authors of the papers in the Women, Risk and AIDS Project (WRAP) collections (Thomson and Scott, 1991). When young women learn that their sexuality is meant to be experienced as passive and responsive in relation to male activity, they learn to suppress their own experience of active sexual desire and to pretend. This learned passivity then leads to an alienated experience of sex and to an incapacity to talk about and negotiate sexual practice, including negotiations about contraception.

Research studies such as those undertaken by WRAP form a useful basis for project work with young women's groups. They help to clarify some important starting points and principles for sex education, for example. There are now a number of possible ways in which girls who grow up hetero-sexual can imagine themselves sexually active and able to take initiatives and make choices about their relationships with boys. The connotation of 'slag' or 'prostitute' still surrounds the image of sexually active women, even when, like Madonna, they are initially seen as strong and independent. However, the transformation in women's lives brought about by access to reliable con-traceptives and to abortion, as well as, more recently, by discussions of 'safer sex' in relation to AIDS, cannot be underestimated.

The interaction between academic study and the work of informal educa-tion with girls has been very evident in the past in a number of areas, includ-ing the work of understanding sexuality. For example, the work of Sue Lees analysed the use of the terms 'slags' and 'drags' in the construction/control of female sexuality (Lees, 1986). This theme of the sexual double standard was taken up and explored in many girls' groups. The poster from the 'Us Girls' poster series' 'We hate you when you call us slags', appeared in youth projects around the country.

Currently, some of the work on popular culture undertaken in the 1980s – particularly Ros Coward's *Female Desire* (1984) and Judith Williamson's *Consuming Passions* (1986) – offers a highly readable and accessible resource for understanding the construction of female sexuality, and for acknowledg-ing the pleasures of heterosexuality. The work of WRAP has focused on the ways young women do or do not negotiate about sex with boys, and to some extent highlights the dangers of heterosexuality. They see the question of control/ being out of control in sex as a part of the construction of heterosex-uality, and they see this as a complex and contested process:

> Women are both sexually subordinated by men, and drawn into the con-stitution of heterosexuality as male dominated in part through the efforts they put into the passive construction of femininity which effectively silences their own desires. (Holland et al., 1994, p.27)

The authors of the WRAP papers are concerned to support a more active fem-ininity in which girls can and do name our own desires. There is a recognition that, to some extent, the sexual health of young women and young women's ability to prevent pregnancy through the effective use of contraception will depend on the encouragement they have to name and acknowledge their own sexual desires. Informal education can clearly offer this encouragement.

The WRAP studies build on feminist discussion of sexuality which devel-oped from Adrienne Rich's powerful essay 'Compulsory Heterosexuality and Lesbian Existence' (Rich, 1980). In this essay, Rich offered a detailed exposure and critique of the forms of heterosexuality available to women, and the forms of resistance to it. Rich developed a definition of the term 'lesbian' which rescued the discussion of female sexuality from the sexologists. Like heterosexuality, lesbian sexuality is also a social construction, produced as a moment of resistance to compulsory heterosexuality or a refusal of it. She offers a model of woman-identified sexuality which reconnects love, desire and resistance. Rich has been rightly criticised for making the term 'lesbian' so broad as to fail to recognise the particular, outlawed nature of female–female sexual desire and practice, and for romanticising relationships between women as free from domination. It is still important to value Rich's identification of female sexuality and female bonding as a source of empowerment and resistance.

Female sexuality: The erotic as power

The phrase 'the erotic as power' is drawn from work of the African-American lesbian poet Audre Lorde. Her account of the female erotic is not limited to lesbian experience, although it finds its focus there, and is one of the clearest expressions of the power of sexuality which is not alienated or made into a commodity for profit-making:

> For as we begin to recognise our deepest feelings, we begin to give up, of necessity, being satisfied with suffering and self-negation, and with the numbness that so often seems like the only alternative in our society. Our acts against oppression become integral with self, motivated and empowered from within.
>
> In touch with the erotic, I become less willing to accept powerlessness or other supplied states of being which are not native to me, such as resignation, despair, self-effacement, depression, self-denial. (Lorde, 1984, p.58)

Such an approach to the erotic for women, including young women, means moving away from a central focus on the negotiations of heterosexuality towards a sense of autonomy in our own bodies and our own desires. The authors of the WRAP papers suggest that the dominant constructions of femininity are, in fact, disembodiments: they remove smells, hair, fat, fluids, movement; 'Women's material (e.g. hairy, discharging) bodies are taken socially to be unnatural.' They argue that:

> Women's empowerment in confronting men's dominance begins with the ability to reclaim their own experience and claim their own bodies as the site of their own desires. This changes the meaning of sexual encounters and female sexuality. (Holland et al., 1994, pp.34 and 36)

In order to reclaim our own experience and to experience our own desire as autonomous, we need words and imaginations and names which will enable us to do so. We need to be able to imagine, speak about and experience our bodies in new ways:

> Kiss me. Two lips kiss two lips and openness is ours again. Our 'world'. Between us the movement from inside to outside, from outside to inside knows no limits. It is without end.

> How can I say it? That we are women from the start. That we don't need to be produced by them, named by them, made sacred or profane by them. That this has always already happened, without their labours. (Irigaray, 1980, quoted in Humm, 1992, p.207)

Such poetry could inform feminist sex education programmes.

As well as naming our desires in new ways, feminist insights can help us name our bodies and understand them more accurately. Feminist work has encouraged us to develop our understandings of our bodies and not simply to rely uncritically on the accounts of the medical profession. The wonderful work *The New Our Bodies, Ourselves* has a place of honour in every women's centre and project (Phillips and Rakusen, 1989). Because the images of women's bodies which dominate our culture bear a largely alienated relationship to actual women, there exists a tremendous need to learn to live in and accept our own bodies and to understand for ourselves our potential for erotic love, our cycles and our fertility. There is a great deal which girls' work can do in support of such processes, and in doing this, 'we do that which is female and self-affirming in the face of a racist, patriarchal and anti-erotic society' (Lorde, 1984, p.59).

Sexuality as performance

Finally, there is a feminist critique which attempts to reject altogether the dualistic accounts of male and female genders and works against attempts to map sexuality onto gender (Butler, 1989). This work gives voice to a desire to 'fuck with gender' and with all accepted patterns. Here is the tradition of the 'mannish lesbian' and of other dyke identities that are not predominantly bound up with normative definitions of masculinity/femininity.

Instead, thinking about queer sexuality engages with histories of lesbian existence and relationships, with the epistemologies of the closet and with the particular ways in which lesbian, gay and bisexual identities have been formed, acted out, lived and performed in different places and cultures. In one influential account, sexuality is not defined as identity, but as what is performed and acted (Butler, 1989). Much work here makes a connection between lesbian sex and other so-called perverse pleasures. Various forms of consensual sex are celebrated, even when they involve sado-masochism, for example. There is delight in the production of erotica and trangressive images.

Clearly, there is an alliance here between lesbians, gay men and other 'sexual dissidents' who want to be able to practice exciting sex without risking AIDS.

Sexuality as performance and as unconnected with identity is the place for 'bad girls', slags and dykes, who delight in having transgressive fun. It is also, like the gay liberation movement and women's liberation movement previously, the place for spectacle and street theatre; a place which allows lesbians to claim a social and political identity, without necessarily accepting a minority status and pleading for 'tolerance' from the majority. In claiming a social and political presence, it builds on the feminist history of connecting the politics of sexuality and the politics of civil liberties. Women who had survived illegal abortions and who took to the streets in support of abortion rights made sexuality a civil liberties issue as 'Pride' does today.

Although much of the agenda of 'queer politics' is male-dominated and does little to challenge women's subordination or promote the emancipation of women, it does nevertheless offer and create a stage on which questions of the varieties of lesbian identification can be explored (McIntosh, 1993).

In this respect, current 'queer' politics seems to be building on earlier lesbian and feminist commitments to 'a woman's right to define her own sexuality'.

How do women workers educate girls about sexuality?

Learning about sexuality through discussions of popular culture

The important place of projects focusing on visual images and on the romance narratives of popular culture has already been mentioned. The relationship between informal education on questions of sexuality and the work undertaken by the teenage magazines is of great significance. The 'problem page' has an honoured and useful place in discussions of the perils of emergent heterosexuality. The genre is easily imitated and has instigated many useful discussions of relationships.

The method simply involves the worker buying up-to-date copies of the magazines, reading out the letters and inviting a small group of young women to discuss them with her. Recent copies of *Mizz* and *Just Seventeen* include discussion on 'why sex is scary' and what to think about before you have sex for the first time, sexual abuse by a grandfather, not wanting to have sex when your boyfriend does, having a crush on someone, feeling ashamed of your body, and 'falling out of love' with someone. Reading aloud tackles the problem of different levels of literacy among young women, and it also allows the worker to gauge young women's reactions and make a 'safe' choice of topic.

If the worker can work with a small group to build on already existing trust and friendship, she will, from this small beginning, readily build up an atmosphere in which a positive sex education programme can develop. It is, of course, very important that the worker herself is well informed on the issues she is tackling, and is supported by knowledge of and access to local family planning services, the attitude to abortion in her local GP network and information about local young lesbian groups. By law, anyone who wants contraception can get it, including access to the 'morning-after pill'. In 1985, a court case decided that young women under 16 had a continued right to get help and advice with contraception. However, recent reports have suggested that access, for example, to the 'morning-after pill' may vary in rather the way that access to abortion services has varied from region to region, and it is essential that youth workers make themselves well informed about the local situation.

Teenage magazines are also important as a source of evidence of the ways in which heterosexuality is constructed as a form of learned ignorance of our own female sexualities and bodies. In 1986, Melanie McFadyean, then the 'agony aunt' for the girls' magazine *Just Seventeen*, described her mailbag: she was at that time receiving some 1000 letters a month from girls aged between 12 and 18 expressing fear and ignorance about their bodies on a range of topics including menstruation, sexuality, relationships, contraception and sexually transmitted diseases (McFadyean, 1986).

Soap operas also offer a useful focus for discussions on sexuality, although the outlandish storylines may make the attempt to connect with young women's daily lives much harder. *Brookside* offered access to an image of lesbian sexuality which is not abhorrent, through the character of Beth Jordache. Such characters will assist girls' workers in building up a repertoire of group discussions about sexuality, which has proved in many cases a successful starting point for further work. Although the plot in which Beth Jordache appears is extremely fanciful, her fictional diaries have become a bestselling book.

One of the methods workers have used for working with material from soap operas, alongside the sort of focused discussion groups mentioned in relation to problem pages, include the creation of storyboards and dramas based on the characters involved. Through such activities, the focused conversation with a purpose which is one of the main skills of youth and community work can occur.

Popular music is rooted in its rhythms and lyrics in the erotic dimension of our lives. It can offer young women and women workers both dreams to live in and nightmares to escape. It is one of the primary means through which many young women interpret their experience, and as such offers a further resource for workers. Workers have made tape compilations with a range of music popular within the groups of young people they are working with as a resource for beginning discussions about the complex relationship between gender, race and sexuality.

Learning about sexuality through a process called 'coming out'

Work on the cultural construction of female sexuality – by working with the readily-available resources of the popular media – can often lead to difficult questions about the worker's own sexuality and sexual practice. Workers often feel very isolated and vulnerable when faced with challenging questions about their sexuality from a group of young people, and as a result react badly. It is essential that there is some discussion in worker teams about the pressures to be personally revealing.

There are both advantages and disadvantages to appropriate self-disclosure, and it is generally not helpful for workers to be more revealing to young people than they are able to be with one another. There are a number of questions which may act as triggers – 'Are you married?', 'Are you on the pill?', 'Have you ever used/seen a female condom?' – but perhaps the most challenging for its implications for the rest of the work of education on female sexuality is: 'Are you a lesbian?'

Teenage popular culture, like academic developmental psychology, tends to suggest that while friendship should never be rejected and must be worked at, it is inevitably subordinate to the girlfriend–boyfriend relationship. The following exchange from the advice page of *Just Seventeen* is fairly standard:

> A few months ago, my friend started going out with this really nice guy. The problem is, we used to be really close (we've been pals since the age of seven), but lately I've begun to feel like I'm losing her to her boyfriend. (*Just Seventeen* fan (14), Birmingham)

> Just because your friend has a new boyfriend and your friendship has changed, it doesn't necessarily mean that you are going to lose her. However, I think that you will have to accept that friendships have to change if they are going to grow and survive. Your friend may not be as close to you as she once was, but this doesn't mean you can't be friends anymore. (*Just Seventeen*, July 1994)

Informal education with girls and young women implicitly and explicitly challenges this sense of priority. The question of whether girls' work is inevitably concerned with work with young lesbians is one which has been widely discussed, since Mica Nava first published her essay 'Every-one's views were just broadened' (Nava, 1992) .

The presence of lesbian workers at the heart of good practice in girls' work should be clearly acknowledged and recognised. Strong female friendship does offer a basis from which both girls and women workers can question 'the heterosexual presumption'. As Mica Nava pointed out, there is, however, often a strong taboo against exploring the erotic dimensions of such friendships which makes discussion of lesbian identification difficult. The fear of being labelled 'lessies', with all the hostility which can still be loaded into that label, is one of the elements which can prevent young women taking part in separate girls' activities.

'Coming out' is a process which is linked to gay identity-formation. Most of the writing on this subject is preoccupied with the male experience, and most of the available accounts describe strikingly similar patterns of growth and change as a mark of homosexual identity-formation. Firstly, they emphasise the context of stigma in which gay identity is formed. Secondly, gay identity is seen to emerge over a protracted period and to involve a number of growth points or stages. Richard R. Troiden suggests a 'four-stage model' including sensitisation, identity confusion, identity assumption and commitment. 'Coming out' therefore, can be seen as a culmination of growing pride in identity and as a highly-charged process in the strengthening of gay identity. 'Coming out' in Troiden's version, occurs at a number of levels and over a period of time. There is a continuum which involves 'coming out' to self, to other gay men and lesbians, to heterosexual friends, to family, to co-workers and to the public at large.

The existence of social stigma against lesbian identity means that the process of gaining a positive lesbian identity can rarely occur in a smooth way. Young lesbians may go out with boys in a response to peer pressure and in an attempt to conform. They may indulge in promiscuous heterosexual behaviour in order to prove themselves straight, sometimes becoming pregnant. Young women involved in same-sex intimate relationships have to keep them secret. So, young lesbians have little opportunity for 'social education' in gaining a positive lesbian identity. 'At a time when heterosexual adolescents are learning how to socialise, young gay people are learning how to hide' (Hetrick and Martin, 1984, quoted in Schneider, 1989, p. 128). Equally, it is very difficult for young lesbians to gain a positive sense of the place of intimate relationships in the whole of their lives. Margaret Schneider expresses this very clearly:

Being a lesbian means being strong, secretive, non-conforming. It is full of contradictions. It means being different and simultaneously being the same. 'The most important unimportant issue' captures the ultimate contradiction in coming out: that the characteristic 'lesbian' is a private, personal issue, far from being the mainstay of identity; yet it becomes a central focus for organising identity and life-style as the result of the need to hide, lie and to be accepted. (Schneider, 1989, p.219)

A woman who has the confidence and strength and makes the choice to come out as a lesbian at work contributes greatly to strategies for combating homophobia. In 'coming out' at work, she allows issues of sexuality to become open, including a more open-ended approach to heterosexuality, as not all heterosexual relationships and households conform to a single pattern. It is also clearly the case that the benefits for young women who are questioning heterosexuality and exploring the possibilities of same-sex relationships are enormous, because a lesbian worker who operates as part of a team and is 'an ordinary, everyday person' offers a potential role model and a public focus for the possibility that lesbians can integrate the public and private aspects of their lives.

However, it will never be safe for lesbian workers to be open about their identities and relationships unless the whole problem of homophobia is addressed within worker teams. 'Coming out' as a strategy needs to apply to all workers, including a 'coming out' about fears and uncertainties in relation to lesbian identification for girls. It means acknowledging a diversity of sexualities within heterosexual and lesbian identifications, and a variety of lifestyles and patterns of household. It means not privileging the two-parent, heterosexual nuclear family as the best family form.

The issue of bisexuality, now emerging as a further positive identity rather than as a 'transition phase', needs to be discussed. It means women being prepared to locate their sexuality on a continuum, rather than in one of two opposed camps. It means everyone being aware of the impact of anti-lesbian legal processes and the social disadvantage and frequent oppression of lesbians, so that pressures and choices surrounding lesbian identification can be explored in a positive way. It means discussion about the place of sexuality and sexual uncertainty in the transition from girlhood to womanhood. It means being clear about guidelines on sex education that govern the work with young people of school age. And it involves a willingness to affirm female sexuality without reference to men.

When it is not possible even to imagine these discussions occurring in a workplace, lesbian workers will continue to feel very threatened and unsafe when working with groups of young women. An alternative, more defensive strategy may be to create a closet for everyone, so that, as a matter of principle, no workers discuss their sexuality or sexual practice, insisting that young women must set their own terms and agendas. The women workers then aim to act purely as facilitators and sharers of objective information.

Support to girls who are 'coming out' can be undertaken either in the context of a young women's group or by making connections with a young lesbian group. Despite the fears surrounding the notorious Section 28 of the Local Government Act 1988 which legislated against local authorities 'promoting homosexuality', young lesbian groups have now been established in a number of areas, including in a number of rural areas.

Suzanne, a member of the Young Lesbian Group in Manchester, describes their group in the following terms:

> The Young Lesbian group has been running for three years. It's run once a fortnight on a Thursday night, it starts at seven and ends at nine. On some nights we have discussions for example about relationships and HIV and Aids. On other nights we socialise, play pool, table tennis, listen to music or have a chat about the latest gossip. Usually, when new members come to the group we meet them before at six forty five. A volunteer and a member go down to meet whoever they are meeting.
>
> The purpose of the group is to be friendly and non-prejudiced. We all tend to have a good time. (Suzanne, Manchester Young Lesbian Group, 1992, p.2)

Young lesbian groups are irreplaceable in offering exactly the kind of opportunities for acceptance and exploration which young women who are growing up heterosexual expect to take for granted.

Sex education/education about relationships

This has long been central to youth work practice, and there is a great deal which women who work in informal education can offer to thinking currently being undertaken in the context of Department for Education guidelines for sex education in schools.

Good practice here can involve work in a number of areas, often undertaken with groups that are well-established and able to trust one another, and using residential work or closed-group work as a method. Sex education programmes and health education programmes clearly offer a positive focus, as do the important themes of female friendship and hopes for the future.

Sex education in schools is now guided by Circular No. 5/94, which interprets the provisions of the Education Act 1993 on sex education, and it is advisable for projects to develop their own policy in relation to sex education, especially regarding permission from parents when working with girls of school age. The 'moral framework' presented in the guidelines is not very hospitable to homosexuality:

> The Secretary of State believes that schools' programmes of sex education should therefore aim to present facts in an objective, balanced and sensitive manner, set within a clear framework of values and an awareness of the law on sexual behaviour. Pupils should accordingly be encouraged to

appreciate the value of stable family life, marriage and the responsibilities of parenthood. They should be helped to consider the importance of self-restraint, dignity, respect for themselves and others, acceptance of responsibility, sensitivity towards the needs and views of others, loyalty and fidelity. And they should be enabled to recognise the physical, emotional and moral implications and risks of certain types of behaviour and to accept that both sexes must behave responsibly in sexual matters. (DfE, 1994, p.6)

The government does, however, recognise the need for education to prevent the spread of AIDS, and the AVERT pack has now become a widely-used resource to offer education on sexual practice to girls and young women (Aggleton et al., 1990). There are always difficulties associated with finding a language for sex. This is particularly so for women, whose genitals have long lacked a sayable name.

Affirmative work with girls about sex is connected firstly with confidence-building. Girls are entitled to and deserve every encouragement to enjoy sex, to experience sex safely and without risk of unwanted pregnancy, and to refuse to participate in sexual activities which are neither safe nor enjoyable. Many of the activities undertaken as part of girls' work programmes contribute to this basic aim of building up confidence.

Secondly, girls are encouraged to find an appropriate language in which to explore and talk about their bodies and desires. Street language for sex, and particularly for the female genital area, is often either vague and inaccurate or carries powerful derogatory connotations. Medical, professional language often seems distanced and alienated: in the same ways that medical diagrams seem to distort our own particular bodies, making our bodies seem wrong. Sex education is based in a process of naming, in which this disembodied and alienated language is laughed about and shouted about, and young women's feelings about particular words and the associations they give to their bodies can be expressed. Once this has been done, young women are encouraged to choose and use their own words, and to understand the pleasures and potentials associated with them. Re-connecting the language we use about our bodies with pleasure and joy rather than with put-downs is enormously empowering. The actual words which are used in the end scarcely matter. Words as different as 'flowers' and 'cunt' have been owned by young women as words for the female genital area. It is the process of exploring meaning which makes the words empowering rather than alienating.

Finally, sex education with girls and young women refuses to separate discussion about sex from discussion about relationships. Possessiveness, love, jealousy, monogamy and control and desire are all themes worth exploring in the context of sex education with girls and young women. The provision of information about the law on abortion, and the ethical debate about abortion, is an important area of work. Pop music has been used successfully to introduce such themes, preoccupied as it is with sex and sexual relationships between men and women. Sex education is about words and talking, because in sex education, we can explore the connection between what we want and what we do. In all this, the mouth, the tongue and the voice are the most important and powerful of organs.

Learning about racism and female sexuality

So far, this chapter has assumed that there are clear common issues about female sexuality across cultures and communities. However, popular culture offers clear distinctions between the sexuality of White European women and of Black women. Women of African descent and women from Asia are subjected to a different range of representations, and are often set up in contrast to one another and in opposition to the dominant norms of White European beauty. It is important that this colouring of our experience of our sexuality is acknowledged, so that negative and destructive accounts either of the 'wildness' and 'savagery' or of the 'passive sensuality' associated, in a racist imagination, with dark-skinned women can be named and resisted (hooks, 1992).

The sense in the dominant culture that Black female sexualities are uncivilised and uncontrolled, and that the 'whiteness' of the 'English rose', in contrast, is civilising, pure and motherly, connects directly to such practices as the prescribing of potentially dangerous contraceptives such as Norplant and Depo Provera to young Black women, who, according to the ideology, cannot be trusted to control their own fertility. Informal education needs to be very aware of these practices and help young women gain confidence in becoming assertive with medical professionals about such issues.

The question of the link between female friendship and autonomous female sexuality and of lesbian identification is likely to occur differently in different cultural groups. Among communities where the separation of the sexes is seen as highly appropriate and in no way detrimental to patriarchal heterosexuality, including most Asian communities, separate work with women does not automatically connect with discussions of the choices about same-sex relationships.

There are a variety of ways in which marriage and motherhood are linked. Sexual practice and motherhood outside marriage are viewed differently by different communities. And understandings of the transition from girlhood to motherhood – particularly associated with different understandings of marriage – make understandings of heterosexuality varied and also mean that same-sex friendship and women's space and community are understood and valued in a variety of ways. For instance, there is a strong assumption of the appropriateness of separate work among many communities, particularly those from South Asia and also from rural African communities. This means there is little barrier to separate work with girls and that same-sex friendships may flourish. However, there is, at the same time, a very powerful taboo against explicit discussion of sex and sexuality, even among communities, with much less disembodied, more sensual cultures and resources than those offered by dominant European cultures. In some Black communities there is the assumption that lesbian identification is a 'White problem', a form of corruption which derives from an acceptance of European values. Black lesbians face both the possibility of homophobia in their own communities and the certainty of racist hostility outside their own communities. This makes the whole process of 'coming out' for White lesbians unlike the process for lesbians from Black communities (Parmar, 1989).

The methods which workers use to develop education about sex and sexuality with young Black women are, of course, the same or similar in many respects to those outlined earlier in this chapter. The resources of popular culture are still worked with, although it may be more difficult to identify resources from popular culture given the extent of the invisibility of Black women in the dominant culture. Other independent cultural resources can be drawn on: the work of the independent film-maker Pratibha Parmar, who was for a long time involved with the development of work with girls and young women, springs to mind, as does the music of Salt-N-Pepa, the female rap artists, and the growing sector of women's magazines aimed at Black women. Project workers will not, on the whole, find such material 'ready to hand' in the way that material which deals with White women's sexuality can be found. With the exception of work in the area of pop music, the cultural resources for positive work with young Black women have to be created. They cannot be reached down from the shelf in packages made earlier.

In this context, too, it is important to recognise the strengths of minority cultures, including family networks and religious traditions which may initially appear hostile to the development of young women's autonomous understanding of sexuality.

Islam, in particular, has been depicted as exceptionally hostile to women. Women workers who themselves share a Muslim background and can recognise the strengths the tradition can offer women can also contribute to the development of the tradition and community in ways which assist young women growing up in Britain. They can be critical within their own community, without sharing in the hostility of the dominant Christian culture. Dominant representations of non-European cultural attitudes to female sexuality often single out practices which seem 'strange' or 'barbaric'. The 'arranged marriage issue' and 'the issue of genital mutilation' are the most obvious.

Any alliance between White feminists and Black women around issues of women's autonomy and choice will be most effective when it is based on support to young women from Black communities developing their own agendas. These agendas may well be concerned with issues within their own communities and in the wider society, and young women will not accept automatically either the terms set by their parents or the terms set by a dominant racist culture.

The importance of policy and learning about sexuality through a civil rights agenda

Government guidelines and fear about what may or may not be permitted in this area is a major inhibitor on good practice. It is very important that projects and organisations working in the informal education sector develop policy and procedures for their work, in line with current policy and practice being undertaken in schools. In recent years, there has been a good deal of policy development in this area. Some is undoubtedly positive, particularly in the discussion of education about sex and sexuality as part of the whole curriculum. However, there is also a good deal of evidence of moral panics, particularly in relation to homosexuality, and although the notorious Section 28 of the Local Government Act 1988 does not apply to schools, it has been widely used as a reason not to support projects aimed at young lesbians and young gay men. Section 2A of the Act states:

2A – (1) A local authority shall not -
(a)   intentionally promote homosexuality or publish material with the intention of promoting homosexuality;
(b)   promote the teaching in any maintained school of the acceptability of homosexuality as a pretended family relationship by the publication of such material or otherwise.

There is no evidence that Section 28 can be used legally to prevent education about sexuality. At the same time, the existence of such legislation clearly reinforces the social stigma associated with lesbian identification and may itself be a powerful justification for the need for young lesbian groups. Same-sex relationships are still much less legitimate than heterosexual ones, and the question of the age of consent for gay men or the rights of lesbians to adopt and foster are just two of the most widely-publicised issues.

If lesbians and gay men are understood as a minority within society, they are entitled to the rights of tolerance and protection which the human rights agenda extends to minorities (Herman, 1994). That the rights of lesbians are so little protected is certainly a theme for political education within young women's groups, and education about sexuality can become an education about civil liberties as well as an education about identity. The young women who shout 'We're here, we're queer and we're not going shopping!' during

'Pride' are clearly involved in a process of empowerment from which informal educators may yet have much to learn. Lesbian Avengers, the direct action movement committed to the defence of the rights of lesbians, has principles of enjoyment, being able to disagree, not making suggestions you are not able or prepared to carry out, and when you disagree, being required to come up with an alternative – principles every community project committed to taking action to defend liberties might adopt.

Female sexuality, whether directed towards women or to men as the object of desire, continues to be caught in the webs of social and political power. Access to abortion continues to be contested and debated. Safe contraceptives are not guaranteed, any more than the right to kiss another woman on the street and not be harassed for it. While this situation continues, education about sexuality will continue to be a political issue, and will continue to be, to some extent, an education in a civil rights agenda.

6 Poverty and motherhood

The attack on single parents

In September 1993, at the height of the government's anti-single mother campaign, the *Panorama* programme on the BBC broadcast a report, 'Babies on Benefit'. The National Council for One-Parent Families took their complaints about the programme to the Broadcasting Complaints Commission and won. The Broadcasting Complaints Commission found in their favour on six separate counts, including the editing of interviews with individual young mothers and the portrayal of a young, unmarried mother of four children to two different fathers as typical. The most important political issue on which the programme focused was that of welfare benefits. The programme claimed that the birth rate in New Jersey had been halved when welfare benefits and access to housing for single mothers were cut. This was not true. On 13th September 1994, Anne Spackman, Chairwoman of the National Council for One-Parent Families, wrote in the *Independent on Sunday* an article entitled 'Feckless or not? The one-parent panorama. We complained and we won':

> The New Jersey Programme combined the carrot of education, work training and childcare with the stick of capping the benefit of any single mothers who had additional children while on welfare. According to the state governor, all these measures together reduced the birth rate to single mothers by 16 per cent.

It is in the context of this public debate that young women living in poverty are expected to raise children. The success of so many women in retaining a sense of purpose and worth as mothers in these conditions is nothing short of a miracle.

Projects working on informal education programmes with young women often have a sense of extreme powerlessness in relation to the economic issues which affect young women's lives. It is therefore tempting to ignore the level of material oppression which affects many young women, and concentrate on other areas of work where projects seem able to have more impact. However, in working with young women, for example, in relation to issues of choice about contraception and abortion and in relation to the experience of motherhood, it is of the utmost importance that projects do not misunderstand the economic and social context in which their work is occurring.

Theorising about 'the underclass'

In the public debate about health, welfare and motherhood, the voice and perspective of the 'underclass' theorists can be heard very clearly, and it is influencing job descriptions, aims and purposes. By 'underclass theorists', I mean the group of economists and sociologists associated with the radical Right and published in this country by the Institute for Economic Affairs, centred around the work of Charles Murray (1994). Although there are also social critics on the Left of the political spectrum, such as Frank Field, who use the concept of the 'underclass' to draw attention to poverty and to offer a much less moralistic and pathologising anti-poverty strategy, the term, on the whole, is deeply pejorative and contains an analysis of poverty which blames the poor themselves for their economic position.

Charles Murray's latest contribution to the debate, in *The Bell Curve*, returns to the old, and many had thought discredited, project of attempting to find a genetic explanation for the distribution of wealth (Herrnstein and Murray, 1994). Extracts from Murray's work have been regularly published in *The Sunday Times* and influence the thinking of policy-makers and politicians who are designing the welfare programmes under which youth work is increasingly funded. For example, many projects are now funded under the rubric of the Health of the Nation agenda, which identifies as one of its targets the reduction by half of pregnancies in girls under 16 by the year 2000.

Of course, not all strategies to achieve the Health of the Nation targets need focus on the 'unhealthy' behaviour of the young. One target aims to reduce the suicide rate among young men, and recent reports suggest that of the many causes of depression among the young, the fear of unemployment rates very highly (DoH, 1992). Yet the opposing perspective to that of the 'underclass' theorists – which focuses not on the culture of the poor, but on the culture of contentment and on the need to attack poverty, create employment and redistribute wealth – is rarely voiced very clearly. The 'underclass theorists' of the new Right have a very explicit concern to establish traditional gender roles. The attention to gender from their critics is often rather minimal.

This chapter is concerned with the work of women in projects which acknowledge the impact of poverty. It is also concerned with survival strategies for feminist practice in projects which are funded and resourced by bodies whose aims are highly consonant with a conservative political commitment to re-educate and re-moralise the poor. It will consider the debate about poverty and the construction of teenage single motherhood as a social problem, and then focus on a number of positive strategies which have been developed to counteract this agenda.

The transition to adulthood for girls

The transition to adulthood for both girls and boys has traditionally been understood as a transition to normal heterosexuality. For boys, this has usually been linked to the transition to adult status as a worker. For girls, the transition to adult heterosexuality has consistently been linked to adult status as a mother. Indeed, motherhood has been represented as the pinnacle of female development, the most prized female identity (Erikson, 1968). This means that for young women living in poor communities – communities where there is a low level of post-16 education, where unemployment levels are high and dependence on social security benefits is common – their experience of the transition to adulthood is marked both by a lack of material resources and also by the attention of middle-class professionals, including journalists and politicians, which sees them as 'problems' when they become mothers at a young age.

The argument here is not that women in poor communities become mothers at a young age in order to secure access to social benefits, as Murray has suggested, but that other routes to adulthood – such as access to employment and further education – are less available than in other European countries with lower rates of teenage pregnancy. So it seems that if young women are to achieve adult status in Britain, their main chance of doing so is through motherhood. Sex education programmes are more contested and more difficult to implement in Britain than in the Scandinavian countries, where the rates of teenage pregnancy are comparatively low (Selman and Glendinning, 1994/5).

So, in responding to the experience of both chosen and unwanted pregnancies and in responding to the experience of becoming a mother, young women are making choices about ways of becoming an adult. Ann Phoenix, in her book, *Young Mothers?* argued:

> Although teenage women who become mothers are often believed to constitute a social problem, it may be more accurate to view them as a group of mothers with problems – often not of their own making – who are struggling against the odds. (Phoenix, 1991, p.253)

Indeed, when benefit levels available to single parents are taken into consideration (the so-called 'welfare incentives' which Charles Murray believes are the problem) – £47.50 a week, plus a 'premium' of £5.10 a week for each child – it is truly a miracle that there are so many young women in poor communities who achieve so much with their children.

This focus on the problem of teenage mothers is closely linked to discussions of the family. Poor White families are pathologised – as 'Negro' families have been in the United States – in relation to the White, middle-class cultural norm.

The ways in which middle-class attention has defined young single mothers in poor communities as a social problem are elaborate and yet condensed into a single, powerful metaphor, in which many of the fears of middle-class culture find a home. All the ways in which young women can be seen as a problem can be expressed in the language of 'risk' and 'trouble' (Hudson, in press; Griffin, 1993). Teenage mothers are seen as a problem, as at risk or in trouble, in a number of different ways.

The problem may be seen to be a moral one: single parents have failed to enter into appropriate commitments, to wait until marriage for sexual intercourse and/or to have children only in the context of a marriage. There is also a medical discourse about single parenthood. This is based on discussions of achieving contraceptive compliance, and the problem appears to be seen as one of stupidity. There is the issue of dependence on welfare benefits. Here the problem is seen to be twofold: firstly, a moral problem of the absence of work ethic where families depend on benefit; secondly, the financial problem of costs to the Welfare State, and of housing costs in particular. There is a discourse about the responsibility of fathers. In the work of the Child Support Agency, this was largely linked to financial settlements and making fathers pay. Women claiming Income Support were threatened with benefit deductions of £8 a week for failing to reveal information about their children's father. The problem became mothers' inability to make fathers stay. A further development of the theme of the absent father is 'out of control' and 'criminal' sons. Mothers who are already perceived as inadequate are now portrayed as responsible for the delinquency and truancy of their sons, and, by association, as responsible for the rising crime rate. Lone teenage mothers cannot be relied on to socialise male children.

Having promoted the free-market economics which announced the triumph of individualism during the heyday of Thatcherism, the Institute of Economic Affairs has now turned its attention to the breakdown of communities – blaming family forms, in particular the feminist demand for greater economic participation and that great shibboleth, 'the 1960s', for the breakdown of community and in particular the rise in crime. In *Rising Crime and the Dismembered Family*, Norman Dennis makes the case very explicitly:

The separation of impregnation from pregnancy is a fact which allows the man to escape the consequences of procreation in a way and to a degree that is quite impossible for a woman. These things have always been true in all societies. What is new about ours is that the whole project of creating and maintaining the skills and motivations of fatherhood and of imposing on men duties towards their own children that are as difficult as possible to escape are being abandoned. What is more, for the first time in history on any large scale, the lead in requiring that the project be aborted has been taken by women.

Young men with a short term view of life and hedonistic values have looked on with quiet delight and can scarcely believe their luck. (Dennis, 1993, p.7)

Writers such as Norman Dennis and A.H. Halsey lay great stress on the importance of families in sustaining communities, and these families are conceived of in traditional fashion (see Dennis and Erdos, 1993).

Within public policy in Britain, there seems to be developing quite a high level of consensus on the sexual politics of community, and it is a consensus which re-emphasises women's responsibility as mothers for the whole community, the importance of the family for the education of the individual, and the importance of morality. The burden of expectation is very heavy here, and if and when young women fail to meet those expectations, they will be focused on once more as problems. Most mothers in poor communities already have all too strong a sense of 'the duties they owe' and too little expectation of the rights they should receive. As mothers, they are in a position from which there seems no escape. Lydia Morris cites the findings of D.J. Smith from the Policy Studies Institute very clearly:

lone mothers define themselves out of the underclass only if they get themselves a job instead of devoting themselves to rearing their children ... they are given a choice between two evils: staying at home to look after their children, in which case they become part of an underclass; or going out to work, in which case they are failing to sustain an ideal of motherhood which others seek to impose. (Morris, 1994, p.120)

The impact of policy on 'teenage mothers' in practice

At the beginning of the girls' work movement, there was a strong sense of needing to present motherhood as a problem for girls, just because becoming a mother seemed to preclude all other possibilities. In a memorable article in the *Working with Girls Newsletter*, Jill Dennis attacked what she perceived as a White, middle-class, feminist perspective on motherhood. 'How dare you assume I made a mistake?' claimed that it is not the children or the young women that are the problem, but the lack of resourcing for children and the assumption that motherhood is all that girls are interested in. Jill Dennis argued that in her own West Indian community, there was a long tradition of young women becoming single mothers and surviving with the support of their own mothers. The perceived feminist attack on motherhood seemed like an attack on such communities, and on the strength of mothers within them (Dennis, 1982). Now it is clearly necessary for projects working with young women in poor communities to understand motherhood as a positive option for women. Only then can its difficulties also be explored and the need to provide alternative definitions of the transition to adult status be acknowledged.

Tony Jeffs and Mark Smith have argued that the impact of the change in social policy towards a consistent identification of young people with social problems and social evils has been the development of a control culture, in which, although projects may seem to continue much as before, especially in methods, the imposition of targets via funding bodies has enormously affected the scope of youth work practice:

> Thus NHS agencies will employ informal educators to work with young people in an area after setting targets for the reduction in the number of teenage pregnancies; Development corporations appoint community and youth workers to get young people off the street or 'slim down offending levels'; Fire Services to reduce arson and false alarms; schools to improve behavioural standards and curtail truancy; city challenge funds detached workers to cut vandalism; and housing departments to stem the flow of young homeless in a given locality.
>
> Workers are increasingly forced into modes of intervention located within a tradition of behaviour modification rather than education for autonomy and choice. The new managerialism, imposition of targets and an authoritarian agenda are collectively reconstructing youth related policy and informal education with young people. (Jeffs and Smith, 1994, p.25)

It is important to insist that this control culture does not affect all young people and all youth work initiatives in the same way. It is very clearly and explicitly gendered; and on the whole, the place of girls within it is to control the boys and assist in the construction of communities better able to cope with the effects of long-term poverty. Control is, in part, to be exercised by encouraging girls to continue to care – to care about children, to care about parents and the elderly, to care about contraception, and to care for men. Such themes find expression in new programmes and new projects linked to new sources of funding, particularly from the Home Office and the Department of Health. Even when such projects employ feminist youth workers, the impact of targeted funding is to marginalise feminist thinking and practice which starts from the question of the potential of young women.

Such a process occurred with the appointment of a 'Young People's Clinic Worker – Sexual Health through Peer Group Learning' in Tameside. The project involved a partnership between the youth service and the health authority. Each participant had identified a need for the project. The health authority had carried out a health needs assessment of primary care in family planning services, which recommended more sex education, improved information and awareness of local services, contraceptive services counselling and support work with young people. The community education service had facilitated a young people's health network which had led to the development in peer-group education on sex and sexuality. Both of these local agendas were linked to the Health of the Nation targets to reduce the rate of conception among the under-16s by 50% by the year 2000 and to reduce the incidence of gonorrhoea by 20% by 1995.

On the face of it, there was ample scope within the project for autonomous, feminist work with girls and young women, and sufficient harmony of purpose to appoint a multidisciplinary team of a clinical medical officer, two family planning nurses, a reception worker and a full-time and a part-time youth worker. The overall purpose of the youth worker post was stated as: 'To work within a team in providing a clinic and contribute to the planning and development of effective approaches to sexual health, i.e. design and deliver peer group learning programmes with young people.'

However, it soon became apparent that the basis on which the different services involved in the project measured effectiveness differed greatly. While the youth workers emphasised process, participation and outreach to marginalised groups, such as lesbian and gay young people, the health workers were able to assess their effectiveness in reaching their targets numerically, in relation to the number of condoms issued. Whereas the youth workers were keen to establish separate spaces for young women, including young lesbians, and to encourage them to have some say in the form the clinic was taking, the health workers wanted to encourage the young women to bring their boyfriends, as it was the boys they needed to reach if they were to meet their target of reducing sexually transmitted disease.

In the end, the health service, who had paid the pipers, called the tune, and in the second stage of the project, the youth work post was established with a specific focus on outreach to young men. In this way, the social policy aims of the Health of the Nation initiative and of 'the control culture' are established, despite the presence and best efforts of highly committed feminist workers.

An alternative account of the experience of poverty can be offered

There are, of course, still alternative accounts of poverty to those put forward by the underclass theorists, but all too often, these fail to consider the nature of sexual divisions within poverty, and so the specific needs of women, once more, are not explicitly recognised. In Bob Holman's lecture to mark the 150th Anniversary of the YMCA, 'Urban Youth: Not an Underclass' (Holman, 1994/5), there is a clear, alternative account of the causes of inequality:

- economic policies which tolerate massive unemployment with its associated poverty;
- market policies which lead to low paid jobs;
- social policies which restrict welfare services;
- tax policies which mean that since 1979, the richest 10% have gained an average £87 a week while the poorest have lost £1 per week. (Holman, 1994/5, p.72)

It is worth considering what this means for a young woman caught in the trap set for her, while trying to make choices about motherhood.

Young women, like young men, have been effectively removed from the benefit system between the ages of 16 and 18, and coerced into the YTS system. This means a weekly income of about £35 – the perpetuation of dependency on their families for basic material needs such as food and shelter. In this situation of denial of economic independence and of structural youth unemployment, the argument of the underclass theorists that there is an economic incentive in the status of single parent takes on a quality of fantasy and farce. More resourcing of young women would offer them more choices.

Job training opportunities may not match local employment opportunities. Traditional areas of employment for women, in relatively low-paid jobs, may persist when traditional male employment has been destroyed. A young woman may expect to be both breadwinner and mother in her adult life. Economic development poses some challenging questions for community work practice with young women:

Whilst wanting to open up non-traditional areas of work for women we must not undermine more traditional roles. However, we must ask are women being offered appropriate education/training for them to make future choices?

Do secretarial courses include elements of administration, confidence building, and the idea of future routes into management?

What sort of courses should be provided in areas of high unemployment where most of the existing jobs are low paid and unskilled? Should we train a pool of women e.g. in new technology in the hope that ultimately such jobs will arrive? Will this build up frustration in a woman who completes such a course but can still only obtain unskilled work? Should we provide courses for community development instead? Does this have to be either/or – can courses be developed which enable women to master new technology but initially use these skills in a community context? (Cole, 1989, p.3)

The link between women's employment and motherhood: The low status of 'care work'

The impact of the restructuring of welfare and the dramatic shifts in social policy about care are a critical focus for understanding young women's experience of poverty. Young women are caught both ways. They are expected to undertake those female roles of caring for others, particularly the dependent members of their families, both the young and the old. If they undertake training in the 'care sector' through National Vocational Qualifications (NVQs), they will end up in low-paid jobs and remain dependent on benefits in the form of Family Income Supplement. The need to undertake unpaid caring work forces them into part-time paid work.

On the one hand, young women with children will find it impossible to take up such training opportunities as are offered because of the need to make provision for children. Young women are also much more likely than young men to be involved in caring for their elders, particularly parents and grandparents, on a regular basis. On the other hand, women's work of caring is increasingly being accredited and certified, but with levels of pay which make economic independence a remote posibility.

The YTS programme still remains highly sex-segregated, with the majority of placements in the social care sector being filled by girls (Cockburn, 1987). Many establishments offering nursing and other forms of care – for example, private day nurseries and residential homes for the elderly – now depend on the work of their YTS trainees for the level of service/ staffing they offer.

The establishment of National Vocational Qualifications in 'care' is highly contradictory. On the one hand, what was once women's duty within families is now acknowledged as a 'skill' and is economically rewarded. On the other hand, the levels of pay associated with 'care work' are very low, and this is partly because it remains ghettoised as 'women's work'.

A number of community-based projects now offer training in childcare for women, and the structure of NVQ programmes does seem to offer a basis from which women can build up confidence to approach the world of paid employment. At the same time, there is a risk of reinforcing the low valuation placed on such work by our society and of diminishing women's expectations of their own worth. It is important for community-based informal education to have good links with vocational programmes in further education, so that young women's access to non-traditional job opportunities can be promoted alongside the perhaps easier route of access to training in 'care'.

Young mothers as copers and organisers

The poverty of young mothers is rooted in lack of access to a decent basic income and is often further exacerbated by housing crisis, when there is no longer sufficient or appropriate accommodation in the parental home. Emergency accommodation to respond to the needs of young women who become homeless is still an urgent priority. Despite this, the government is still proposing to amend the Housing (Homeless Persons) Act 1977 to remove priority for young mothers. However, it is important not to regard young women and young mothers as entirely victimised by these circumstances. Young women's capacity to survive and even thrive against these odds is a constant cause for amazement.

Writers like Christine Griffin take a very different view of culture from the view of the underclass theorists – they stress young women's diversity, the range of different experiences of motherhood which young women have and the range of responses that can be made, even in apparently impossible circumstances. She stresses the agency, creativity, resilience and survival which occurs among young women (Griffin, 1993).

It is this kind of response to poverty which prevents projects falling entirely back into a philanthropic model of assistance. Models of self-help and mutual aid are continually redeveloped and sustained by women in poor communities: community associations can facilitate credit unions, which prevent loan sharking in poor areas; food co-ops which buy in bulk can enable people to buy cheaper food (a loaf for 27p rather than 50p, for example); toy libraries enable the sharing of toys for children across neighbourhoods; children's clothes stores allow hardly-worn clothes to be exchanged; sewing classes enable clothes to be made more cheaply; canteens in community associations allow access to cheap and nutritious cooked food. All this is women's work of community organising, and it is important that young women are involved in it. In one community association, young women have organised a nappy co-op, to spread the cost of purchase of disposable nappies!

The role of the woman worker in working with young women in situations of poverty is surely to recognise and nurture such survival activity.

A good example of the networks which develop in the process of community organising is found in the report of the Zion Community Health and Resource Centre in Hulme, Manchester. The report covers HIV/AIDS and drugs, mental health, women and children, training and liaison. The Aisha Childcaring Group, which was established initially to offer training to parents, has become a childcare resource for the whole project:

> They now offer afterschool club, playschemes and sessional creche care. In the past year this has meant that the creche has been open every week for the women's health drop-in and the women's art class. Aisha volunteers

have also been developing training packages and policies to help them cope with issues such as difficult and challenging behaviour, as well as policies on assertive discipline and equal opportunities ... Aisha, Homestart and Children's Services (Manchester City Council) have worked together through the Hulme Health Forum to establish a Toy Library and an Accident Prevention Home Loan scheme. (Zion Community Health and Resource Centre, 1993–4)

Principles of good practice

Bob Holman (1994/5) suggests some essential principles for projects working in poor communities, and I repeat them here with some modifications, because we are concerned here specifically with young women:

1 Work at the hard end. This means not turning away from young women who are most exploited and needy, and also recognising the young women who are ready to take initiatives, and building groups to support them all. It means paying attention to developing a strong project team.
2 Make sure projects are long-term. Short-term, 'targeted' funding and worker teams who come and go cannot really assist community development work with young women. Projects need time to become part of an area. Some of the most successful boys' clubs have been established for more than one hundred years!
3 Make sure projects are available. The life crises associated with stress and poverty do not usually occur during project opening hours. Be prepared to employ workers during 'anti-social hours' and to employ local workers and volunteers to offer emergency support and respite.
4 Share power, and particularly information and decision-making about the project with project users.
5 Be prepared to create opportunities as well as responding to difficulties.

The class division of caring: Feminist practice and the agenda of part-time workers

Because young women are so often regarded as the bearers of problems and responsibilities, they must become accustomed to being seen as individuals in their own right, with their own potential to develop.

At the beginning of the girls' work movement, it was possible for Mica Nava to comment on the possibility of the shared experience of women workers and girls – the shared experience of femininity – being more important than class division.

The need to find common ground and make alliances across class positions is still of primary importance, but the significance of class divisions between women cannot be denied. Nicky Gregson and Michelle Lowe (1994) have convincingly argued that the resurgence of waged domestic labour during the 1980s represents a breakdown of the post-war cross-class identification of women in Britain with all forms of reproductive work. In other words, the re-emergence of servants means one group of women benefiting from the exploitation of other women. Many middle-class women are able to sell their labour power as 'honorary men'. They are no longer physically responsible for all forms of domestic labour. Gregson and Lowe also suggest that certain domestic tasks are becoming closely identified with women from specific classes:

> Thus, whilst the daughters of white collar lower management and secretarial labour constitute a significant facet of the reproductive labour associated with childcare in the homes of the middle classes, the messiest aspects of daily household reproduction are being transferred to working-class women. (Gregson and Lowe, 1994, p.233)

Middle-class girls become nannies, working-class women become cleaners. Salaried women in full-time posts have the privilege of working all the hours that men work, in the same jobs, and paying other women to undertake aspects of 'their' housework. So 'liberation' for some women is being bought at the cost of 'oppression' for others. Strategies of alliance will have to be created to challenge the evaluation of all kinds of caring and reproductive work.

This issue of the class division of caring, in particular as it structures the relationship between part-time, volunteer and full-time workers in informal education and in community work, must be addressed by feminist practice. Women workers with degrees and postgraduate training may find themselves able to command salaries comparable with those of other professionals, while part-time workers are accredited with NVQ type qualifications in informal education and do most of the face-to-face work with girls and young women. Feminist-inspired work must challenge these divisions and differentials.

Feminist trade unionists in the Community and Youth Workers Union were among the first to argue the case for parity of pay and conditions between part-time and full-time workers. This case was finally acknowledged in law as a result of a judicial review in December 1994. Michael Portillo, Employment Secretary, announced to the House of Commons that the different qualifying conditions for part-time workers in relation to unfair dismissal and redundancy payments were to be removed. This will mean that part-time employees will qualify for employment rights on exactly the same basis as full-time workers.

In forming alliances between part-timers and full-timers, and between volunteers and paid workers, it is essential that everyone recognises they have something to gain as women from such alliances. Strategies for assessing good practice or proposals for bargaining and negotiating over pay and conditions were developed which revolved around the question: 'How will these proposals affect the position of a low-paid, part-time woman worker who is also a single parent?' If the proposed strategy had the potential to improve her position, it could be supported as 'in the interests of women members' by the Women's Caucus, which was an autonomous group of women trade unionists within the union structures. For a time, this organising met with some success, even though the right of women to organise autonomously was bitterly opposed by many male (and some female) trade unionists.

The insights gained into the structure of waged employment and its links to the unwaged and voluntary provision of care have the potential to transform social relations between men, women and children. It remains to be seen whether such alliances between part-time and full-time workers can survive the introduction of contract funding. Into an alliance which explores the relationship between waged work and family for women must come an understanding of the growth of self-employment and 'freelancing', as well as new forms of homeworking and 'teleworking'. Without such alliances continuing to be forged, feminist practice will become a strictly elitist activity.

7 Independence and dependency: The politics of disability

There is a cartoon which shows a social worker arriving to meet a young woman who is using a wheelchair, perhaps to prepare her for community care/independent living. The social worker says to the young woman: 'We're going to empower you ... but don't worry, if you can't manage, we'll disempower you again.'

The problem of patronising and overprotective attitudes to young women is probably felt nowhere more acutely than in the experience of young disabled women, and many of the contradictions of women's involvement with care run through young disabled women's lives very sharply. All women are supposed to occupy the contradictory position of being dependent members of households – dependent daughters or dependent wives – and at the same time to be in a position to offer care to others, to meet the needs of dependants. Many of the dominant images associated with disability remove young women from one pole of the contradiction. Disabled women are permanently dependent and needy (when not brave and tragic, and expected to simply carry on coping and caring for others, in their role of superheroes).

In some ways, it seems that disability overrides gender in the eyes of the dominant culture. The signs outside toilets illustrate this graphically: men, wheelchairs, women. People who use wheelchairs are a third category. So, for young disabled women, possibly the first and most important step is to claim to be a woman in the first place, sharing in the constructions of femininity which affect women who are non-disabled too. Strongly positioned as needy and dependent, young disabled women claim their abilities to act as women and care for others, sexually, emotionally and materially. Young disabled women also claim their rights to independence and to non-discrimination.

The perspective of young disabled women is necessary in thinking about informal education with girls and young women, both in its own right and because such a perspective sharply highlights some of the questions of discrimination, of rights to counter discrimination and of the need for independence which inform feminist practice in a number of ways.

The disabled people's movement and the rejection of the medical model

The disabled people's movement – a movement for the civil rights of disabled people – has highlighted many social practices which disable and discriminate. There have been demonstrations and direct action under the campaign slogan 'Rights not charity'; media monitoring and direct action in relation to representation of disabled people by charities such as Telethon and Comic Relief; the emergence of 'disability culture' and a disabled people's arts movement; a political engagement with the 'care in the community debate' from the perspective of disabled people themselves; the success of the Americans with Disabilities Act for the movement in the USA, and the humiliation of the Conservative Party for its public failure to support the Disabled Persons' Civil Rights Bill introduced as a Private Member's Motion by Dr Roger Berry MP in 1994.

In relation to professionals working in social services or in education, probably the major achievement of the disabled people's movement has been to create a shift in understanding away from a medical model: 'What's wrong with you?' – towards a social understanding of disability. It is social structures which disable, far beyond the impact of particular impairments.

This, in turn, should begin to shift understanding away from thinking about 'special provision' for 'special needs' to thinking about how 'mainstream' provision needs to change to enable everyone to participate as citizens of the same society.

Coalition-building among disabled people

The disabled people's movement is a coalition, and anyone interested in the politics of coalition-building has a great deal to learn from its achievements. In Greater Manchester, the main campaigning body is the Greater Manchester Coalition of Disabled People, and in writing this chapter, I have been very much assisted by discussion with the young women's group which meets as part of the Greater Manchester Coalition of Disabled People's youth project.

Workers with the project, Maureen Green, Julia Keenan and the 'trainee' worker, Tracy Yankowski, are keen to point out that while disabled people share common interests, they do not constitute a homogeneous group. Nor do disabled people, any more than any other group campaigning against oppression, miraculously shed their own socialisation in the process of campaigning for change. The young women's project, like many other young women's projects, has arisen partly in response to sexism and partly to affirm disabled young women as women and to create a trusting environment where young women can share experiences.

One of the most impressive aspects of any coalition of disabled people is the attention which needs to be directed to basic communication, to enable access of all participants to the work of a group. This reflects the good practice all too rarely found in group work. Undoubtedly, this attention to process and to access has greatly contributed to the disabled people's movement's success in coalition-building. The women who created *With the Power of Each Breath: A Disabled Women's Anthology* express this clearly. They write:

> The complexities of doing the work in ways that maximised each of our individual strengths, and, at the same time, acknowledged our human limitations and specific disability-related needs were staggering. The material we received had to be available in several forms to be accessible to us all. We needed taped and Braille versions, as well as printed, to communicate with each other. Major fluctuations in our disabilities required us to use different media at different times. The logistics of finding and scheduling readers to tape printed information was a continuous job. But with the help of contributors and friends, tapes, Braille and the telephone, we managed. (Browne et al., 1985, p.10)

In the same way, the young women and workers who formed the young women's group at the Greater Manchester Coalition for Disabled People chose to communicate with great attention. Not everyone in the group has sight. Some members rely on lipreading. Some members' speech is 'interpreted' by others. This slows communication down to a level where all can participate and everyone can be heard, and, as is often the case, slowing communication down can improve its quality. With the help of the youth workers, the discussion on young disabled women's perspectives has focused on some important areas for consideration.

How can a disabled woman achieve adult status?

The question of what is a 'young woman', of transition to adulthood, is formulated slightly differently in each theme approached in this book. Does a young woman become an adult when she becomes a heterosexual? When she becomes a mother? When she gains economic independence or a house of her own?

One of the workers suggested that adolescence is very prolonged for a disabled woman because it is assumed that she will be unable to achieve these adult statuses. She is assumed to have no sexuality, no possibility of forming sexual relationships, and therefore to have no chance of becoming a mother. She may, as a result, remain under the protection of her parents all her adult life, retained in a state of almost perpetual childhood, or she may, perhaps well into her twenties, engage in a period of rebellion against such enforced dependency. The corollary of a long period of unexpressed sexuality may be a period of highly-charged sexuality, expressed in risky and dangerous ways. If she becomes a mother, it is likely to be assumed either that this was a mistake, or that she became a mother before she was disabled, and there is likely to be scrutiny of her fitness to be a mother.

Such scrutiny is based on the perceived reversal of women's duty to be caring. How can a woman who is perceived to be in need of care, to be dependent, offer the kind of permanently-available care which mothers in our kind of society are meant to offer? Will she not come to depend on her children to care for her, in ways which are disadvantaging for them. In the discussion of community care, the plight of 'young carers' – children who care for their parents – has been highlighted. Against the norms of a society in which everyone is meant to be positioned on one side or the other of a weak/strong and helper/helped divide, how can a disabled woman with children be positioned as anything other than a 'problem family'?

This roadblock of disabling assumptions in the way of young disabled women becoming adults, becoming mothers, in the ways other young women do, repays very careful scrutiny. The issues raised by the experience of women disabled from their early life who do become mothers are exciting and challenging. They have an impact on all the debate that needs to occur about how children are to be cared for, whose responsibility it is to provide that care, how children's own desire to care for others is to be nurtured but not exploited. They challenge the role our society gives to professional social workers as 'experts' in the assessment of such issues: a role which then enables everyone else to avoid the debate. Meanwhile, disabled women who do establish sexual relationships and become mothers offer an important example to young disabled women that a transition away from parents or institutions and towards independent living is possible.

The education system as a disabling force

A second major area for discussion is the part played by education in 'robbing you of your rights'. Many disabled young women still experience segregated or 'special' education. The term 'special needs' is particularly disliked. It is felt to disguise the reality of young women's experience of being sheltered and protected, in the framework of lack of opportunity and the expectation that they will have menial jobs or that their impairment will prevent them from achieving. This view of the limitations of special education has been consistently upheld by Her Majesty's Inspectorate of Education, and yet progress towards integrated education provision has been painfully slow. The TUC (1995) statement on civil rights for disabled people records the following.

- Reports on special schools by HMI rated accommodation and resources at best 'satisfactory' to 'downright dangerous'. Other reports have found specialist science facilities rare in the smaller special schools. Special schools often have no teachers with expertise in important subjects, especially science and maths.

- Other official reports have looked at the position of children in mainstream schools. In primary schools, most classrooms have insufficient space for children who use personal aids and equipment, and many schools do not have accessible toilets and changing rooms. In most secondary schools where there are young people with physical impairments, few adaptations have been made. In many cases, inaccessibility prevented students being able to choose major subjects at GCSE.

- A 1987 survey of further education colleges found that fewer than a third were able to offer physical access in all teaching blocks, and more than a fifth said they might have to reject a student 'with a physical handicap' because of poor access or inadequate support. A 1990 survey of polytechnics and universities found a similar picture.

One of the young women in the Manchester disabled young women's group had been prevented from following her chosen training in a GNVQ/BTEC in caring because the nearest college which could offer her access and support to do the course was in Coventry! None of the young women in the group had expressed particularly unusual ambitions in terms of employment – a number were interested in work in the care sector, particularly with children or in social work. Others had interests in gardening and working with computers. Everyone recognised that as a result of their impairments, they might require assistance to undertake courses, or that colleges might need to make adaptations to premises and/or equipment to offer them access to the same opportunities as other young women.

The role of the women workers working with this group was clearly to build up confidence and offer a safe forum in which young women could develop the assertiveness to demand their rights to education within the society of which they are members.

Using anger and tackling harassment and discrimination

Such experience of being denied access to basic social rights, and even of being denied *any* expectation of such rights, inevitably leads to anger, and the manipulation of the many feelings provoked – both in disabled and non-disabled individuals – by the encounter with disability is a major source of difficulty for young women.

In our society, femininity is identified with emotionality, and being appropriately feminine means handling emotions appropriately: your own and other people's. It is probably impossible for a young disabled woman to be 'appropriately feminine', as she is so often a dumping ground for other people's fears about 'normality', weakness and pain. At the same time, she has to cope with her own feelings, both about her impairment and about the treatment she receives. As one of the young women in the Manchester group put it: 'If your confidence is battered throughout your life, you grow up very angry.' Informal education must address this anger, as it is potentially an enormous resource for change:

> Anger felt by women because of our disabilities is rarely accepted in women's communities, or anywhere else for that matter. Disabled or not, most of us grew up with media images depicting pathetic little 'crippled' children on various telethons or blind beggars with caps in hand ('handicap') or 'brave' war heroes limping back to home where they were promptly forgotten. Such individuals' anger was never seen, and still rarely is. Instead of acknowledging the basic humanity of our often-powerful emotions, able-bodied persons tend to view us either as helpless things to be pitied, or as Super Crips, gallantly fighting to overcome insurmountable odds. (Thompson, 1985, p.78)

If the anger produced by such stereotyping can be acknowledged, instead of, as is so common with women, being turned inwards into despair and depression, it will become a powerful force:

> Disabled women must learn to understand their own anger and to accept that it is both reasonable and justified. It is lousy to be disabled and it is perfectly healthy and normal to feel that way, at least occasionally. The trick however is to learn to control that anger so that it does not become a liability in and of itself ... Those of us who are disabled must learn to cope with the anger provoking reality that all those many barriers are not going to come tumbling down all at once, as unjust, unfair and just plain infuriating as they are. It is not easy to have to work our lives around the multitude of obstacles society has put in our way ... We need to find effective coping mechanisms to help us keep sane and strong. For some, political

action may be useful. For others a support group may help. There are numerous possibilities. The important thing is to find a way to survive. (Thompson, 1985, p.78)

The role of anger and of the emotions, especially at a point where young women recognise that their rights as independent persons are effectively being denied, is one of the most important issues in informal education with girls, and it provides one of the places where alliances between girls and women with very disparate experiences may be forged.

Another experience associated with patterns of discrimination is the experience of harassment. Young women at the Greater Manchester Coalition of Disabled People's Youth Project have described the experience of being called names and being bullied, and also the experience of being petted, pitied and talked over: 'People stroke you and feel they have a right to touch you.' For young disabled women, the experience of being touched sexually without their consent appears to be an extension of this objectification associated with disability. The young women's group provides an essential forum in which experiences of bullying and harassment can be identified and named for what they are, and in which young women can swap survival stories and tactics and be as emotional as they need to be.

It seems fairly clear that informal education projects which start from a tokenistic position of including young disabled women in 'mainstream' provision are unlikely to be able to address in the same depth the issues raised by an autonomous group of young disabled women, meeting within the framework of a campaigning voluntary organisation of disabled people, rather than an organisation for disabled people.

Integration – but on whose terms?

'Mainstream' projects must strive for integrated provision, but this must be done on the terms of young disabled women, and with their interests paramount. All too often, it is the needs of the 'mainstream' service to be seen to be doing something that become paramount. Then, the development of policy and awareness can seem in inverse proportion to action taken. Disabled members of 'mainstream' projects are sometimes 'worn like a badge' of the good intentions of the non-disabled workers. 'Integration' or 'mixing' for their own sake can never provide a sufficient purpose and will always, in the end, fail to prioritise sufficiently the interests of the group which has been excluded. The long, and no doubt for many individuals extremely worthwhile history of the PHAB (Physically Handicapped–Able-Bodied) clubs seems to have done little to challenge disabled young people's exclusion. It seems better practice to support disabled workers in establishing autonomous groups and gaining appropriate qualifications, and to build up joint work, including integrated provision, with the human rights agenda in mind.

However, most of the work with young disabled women does currently occur in settings and organisations which are *for* disabled people rather than in organisations *of* disabled people. In these organisations there is an in-built tendency for a model of charity rather than of rights to come to the fore, and it is very important that workers are aware of this.

In 1993, Sue Quinn, Youth Club UK's Disability Development Officer, organised a conference in Lancashire for women workers to examine their practice with young women. One of the projects which presented their working methods was Connect, a Stockport-based project which aims to 'enable disabled young people to develop their own social and leisure lives in whatever way they see fit'. The worker at the project, Caroline McPhee, stated:

> Disabled young women are affected by the same cultural influences as able-bodied young women and should be allowed to take risks and possibly make mistakes to find out what they want to do. (Quinn, 1993, p.24)

Projects can gear their work to opening up new opportunities for disabled young women, particularly, perhaps, in relation to further education provision and to positive action to make up for opportunities denied through schooling.

Gill Whittle, from Merseyside Youth Association's Advocacy Project, focused on self-advocacy, described as being able to make choices and decisions, being able to express thoughts and feelings with assertiveness if necessary, having clear knowledge and information about rights, and being able to effect changes. Here, there is clearly a link to the collective campaigning work undertaken by disabled people's organisations. However, advocacy projects may have a tendency to position young people as weak and vulnerable initially, rather than starting from strength. The charity model can re-emerge in the form of mistakenly low expectations on the part of non-disabled workers.

A third workshop focused on self-defence, the development of self-confidence in young disabled women to deal with the abuse and harassment they so often face, and enabling young women to make their own definitions about personal safety, rather than simply accepting the evaluations of places and situations given them by others (Quinn, 1993).

If thinking such as this, as well as the necessary work of adapting buildings and resources, were to gain a foothold in mainstream services, the project of including disabled young women on the same terms as others would be greatly strengthened.

Some young women's projects have taken positive steps to involve young disabled women in their activities. Getaway Girls in Leeds was established precisely to enable access to adventurous and outdoor activities to girls whom everyone assumes aren't interested in or can't do certain activities. The project took quite a strategic approach, particularly in taking positive action by employing a deaf woman as a trainee worker and supporting her training. This strengthened the project's existing links with deaf girls, and the project then went on to employ a sign interpreter and to offer a signing service. By 1992, the project had proposed a five-year development plan, with a strong emphasis on disability awareness training with mainstream services which discriminate against disabled people.

Self-organisation of disabled youth and community workers

Employment rights are a major focus of attention for the civil rights of disabled people, and if young disabled women are to progress with the work of coalition-building, mutual support and education, greater numbers of disabled women will need to be employed in informal education and community development roles and to become qualified in a range of occupations.

And so the circle is complete. Institutions which offer training, particularly further education colleges and universities, must change their direction and policies to enable access. The desire among women who are aware of the denial of their rights to 'smash the system from the inside' is very strong. Feminist practice should give every assistance to this process. There is now a national network of disabled youth and community workers, established on an independent footing. It is from such an independent network of disabled workers that the essential and necessary role models for young disabled women in the future will emerge.

8 Violence against young women

Recognising and acknowledging sexual violence

The question of violence is never far away in groups of girls and women. Yet the so-called 'disclosure' of the presence of coercion in the lives of the young women who are involved in a young women's group is often greeted with shock. Instead of recognising that some level of coercion is, in fact, normal and everyday, the most common response often suggests that the experience of violence is unusual. A skilful response acknowledges the presence of degrees of force and violence in the everyday reality of many girls and young women, while at the same time stressing the unacceptability of violence in personal relationships.

When the particular circumstances that have led to violence in particular cases are investigated, there are always ready-made explanations available. These can easily distract attention from a common pattern. Violence seems 'alien': 'It could never happen to me.' 'It never happens to me.' Or else it's seen as a product of deviant individuals in deviant relationships: 'He's a bastard, but she loves him.' or 'What a monster! How could they do that to their own children?' Or the young woman who is experiencing violence believes herself to have no connection with other women: 'It only happens to me.' Liz Kelly's important work *Surviving Sexual Violence* (Kelly, 1988) offers a feminist framework for understanding the connections between different kinds of violence which women experience at the hands of men. She identifies the prevalence of a shared ideology about rape, incest/sexual abuse and domestic violence which focuses attention on the victim rather than the perpetrator. For example, in relation to the myth that 'they' (that is, women) 'tell lies/exaggerate', this may be expressed in relation to rape as: 'Women make false reports for revenge, or to protect their reputation.' In relation to incest/sexual abuse, as: 'Girls fantasise about incest, or accuse men of sexual abuse to get attention.' In relation to domestic violence, it is expressed as: 'It wasn't violence, only a fight. Women exaggerate to get a quick divorce.' (Kelly, 1988, p.35).

Liz Kelly argues that this commonsense reversal should point us to a recognition of an ideology: a powerful body of beliefs and ideas which disguise the truth, almost turn it upside down. In this case, it is an ideology which mystifies the recognition of the ways in which men's violence facilitates the social control of women. Kelly sees violence as resorted to only when other forms of control have failed, because the use of violence makes the existence of coercive power evident and so facilitates resistance: 'Male violence arises out of men's power and women's resistance to it' (Kelly, 1988, p.23).

In developing her definition of violence, she begins with the recognition, found in the dictionary definition, that violence involves damage to the self, denial of the victim's will and autonomy, and that such violence may be physical, emotional, psychological. She then extends this to explore the place of sex in men's violence, and the need to include women's own account of what has happened to them in any definition:

> Sexual violence includes any physical, visual, verbal or sexual act that is experienced by the woman or girl, at the time or later, as a threat, invasion or assault, that has the effect of hurting her or degrading her and/or takes away her ability to control intimate contact. (Kelly, 1988, p.41)

Unfortunately, the myths and stereotypes about sexual violence are still very prevalent and affect services offered to women experiencing or escaping violence. All too often, it seems to be the case that the impact of violence is not taken seriously and the difficulties facing women trying to leave relationships are minimised. Attention is turned to trying to get women to change their behaviour. The feminist response to this dominant welfare agenda has been the development of a network of services for women and girls who have been abused. This is largely because of the inadequacies in the response of the statutory agencies and the extent to which myths and stereotypes are reflected in their practice. From the base of these alternative services, campaigning work which challenges definitions, myths and stereotypes has been undertaken to encourage change in public attitudes. There have also been systematic initiatives to challenge practice within statutory agencies.

There have been close contacts and connections between feminists working in Rape Crisis and Women's Aid, for example, and feminists working in community-based projects with girls and young women. The purpose of this chapter is to explore ways in which feminist understandings of violence can lead to ways of working which are not 'firefighting' or 'crisis work'. They can also enable the reality of struggle and survival to be acknowledged. Personal troubles can, over and over again, be identified as public issues. After almost thirty years of feminist activism, the United Nations is being lobbied to include domestic violence alongside torture as an abuse of human rights.

How does sexual violence become apparent to workers?

Forms of violence which may become apparent to workers in the course of running a girls' group or a young women's group include assault, rape, sexual abuse of children by adults, physical abuse of children by adults, racial harassment and racist attacks. There are forms of violence which are administered therapeutically, for example by doctors in the treatment of mental illness. Violence is also directed against the self by young women in the form of self-harm and attempted suicide.

The experience of violence can become apparent in a number of ways. A young woman may arrive at a project displaying her bruises. She may lie about how she came by the bruises. Another young woman may organise herself to take part in a project event, only to find herself prevented from doing so as a result of threats from her partner. Sometimes, there is talk about men arriving home drunk, or of sexual encounters that got out of hand. Among a group of women, the issue of violent threats is often assumed and unspoken, or acknowledged only implicitly: 'You know what men are like, don't you?'; 'He's in a bad mood; you want to keep away from him at the moment.' The worker must then decide how and in what ways to make the issue explicit. She also has to find ways to assert the unacceptability of violence.

At other times, women's experience of violence may emerge as a result of personal conversation with a worker. She may have become desperate to break the silence and let someone know what is happening to her. Or she may have begun to internalise her angry response to violence – turning it in on herself in the form of depression or of suicide threats.

The question of the prevalence of sexual abuse, which has emerged in the context of feminist movements in recent years, has raised awareness of the relationship between self-directed violence and the threats of an oppressive adult exercising sexual power over a child. A child who is made to feel worthless and hateful may begin to behave in ways that reinforce this belief.

When a child or a young woman lets a worker know that she is experiencing violence from adults who are responsible for her care, the worker must be able to recognise and acknowledge her responsibilities to respond to the news she is receiving, however little she wants to hear it. It is important to recognise that girls and young women will give such information to adult women workers because they believe that the adult has more power than they have and can intervene to support them. Information shared in this way is also shared on the basis of trust, and it is essential not to break that trust. All citizens share in a duty to protect children. It is therefore essential that projects develop clear guidelines for workers, rooted in the provisions of the Children Act 1989.

The fact that there is so little published material in relation to the duties and responsibilities of youth workers in this area is a clear indication of the dominance of the male agenda in youth work. In the development of feminist-inspired work in crisis projects, a number of principles for good practice have emerged.

Good practice in acknowledging and responding to women's experience of violence

Firstly, it is important that any woman who begins to talk about her experiences of violence is believed. This simple step is an act of resistance to the myth that all women who report experiences of violence or harassment are liars and prone to exaggeration. It is not a matter of claiming that women and girls *never* lie or make up stories. But the act of believing allows women to make their own claims to truthfulness, to name their own experience, before perhaps having their claims subjected to the scrutiny of the courts or other 'experts'. On the whole, the ideology that women are liars or that we embroider the truth often seems to lead women to disbelieve their own experience or to minimise the harm and hurt we have received, rather than to exaggerate it. There is also the important coping mechanism of forgetting. The existence of 'forgetting' as a coping mechanism and the enormous publicity given to the proponents of 'false memory syndrome' make it even more important that women's own early attempts to name their own experiences and to understand them are believed (Burman, in press).

Secondly, it is very important to listen out for, reject and challenge ideas of self-blame, or the belief that the violence which a young woman experienced was acceptable. The belief that women provoke violence, or are able always to successfully resist if they so desire, is central to the ideology which perpetuates such violence. It has been internalised to some degree by everyone. Women scrutinise their own behaviour, asking themselves: 'What did I do wrong?' In some cases, this amounts to simply a sense of being in the wrong place at the wrong time. As Liz Kelly points out:

That women feel they are responsible simply by 'being there' demonstrates the power of the ideology that women are responsible for men's

violence. That an assault happens at all becomes sufficient reason for
women to feel that they might be at fault. (Kelly, 1988, p.212)

Part of the role of workers is to assist young women in understanding that
they are not responsible for violence committed against them. This is the
beginning of a process of helping women place responsibility for violence
where it belongs: with the perpetrators.

This is clearly linked to the process of building up self-respect once more.
Violence often leads to a loss of self-respect, confusion, depression and breakdown. It is important for workers to be able to affirm clearly and unequivo-
cally that violence is not an appropriate or acceptable basis for intimate
relationships, that what has happened to a young woman is not acceptable,
and that she does not have to accept it.

Thirdly, wherever possible, workers must be prepared to offer alternatives
to a young woman, and choices about how to tackle the situation she is in.
What kind of alternatives are available will depend very much on the age of
the young woman, the statutory responsibilities this places on a worker,
whether she has children who may also be at risk in the situation she is in,
and, most relevant of all, the material resources of housing, respite accommodation and counselling available in the area. However, it is when a young
woman can see and understand an alternative to her current situation that
the pattern of self-blame and loss of self-respect can most successfully be
challenged. Without such material alternatives, the work of self-recovery is
greatly hampered.

Much sexual violence occurs in intimate relationships and occurs 'in the
name of love'. There is a good deal a worker can do here to explore with
young women their understanding of love and, without denying that their
intimate relationships are indeed love relationships, to question whether
love, or even simply the consent to access to another person's body,
inevitably involves hurt. Some groups have developed programmes of
assertiveness training which enable women to clarify for themselves what
they do or do not want from their relationships with others.

Fourthly, workers must respect the trust and confidentiality placed in
them by the young women they work with, without denying the limits
placed on 'in confidence' conversations by the legal responsibilities for child
protection which they, in common with all adults, hold. The Manchester
Youth Service guidelines make it clear that a worker cannot guarantee confidentiality to a young woman who confides in a worker about abuse, and
recommend that workers state this at the beginning of 'in confidence' discussions. This at least has the merit of allowing a young woman to make an
informed choice before deciding to confide.

The importance of partnership

The Children Act 1989 instigated a period in which the necessary partnership between education authorities and social services departments became further reinforced as a legal duty. This duty has two aspects. Firstly, there is a duty to make a regular (three-yearly) review of all provision of daycare and early-years education, in order to ensure that children's needs are met. Secondly, there is a duty to co-operate, under Section 47 of the Act (child protection investigative duty) in the conduct of enquiries by social services departments or the National Society for the Prevention of Cruelty to Children. Any person, including any Local Education Authority (LEA), must assist in such enquiries if called upon to do so, unless it would be unreasonable in all the circumstances of the case. The Department of Health, Department of Education and Science, Home Office and Welsh Office guidelines on partnership are clearly expressed in *Working Together* (DHSS and WO, 1988), and there should be no doubt in the minds of any staff employed, either in an education service, in family and community services or in the health services, of their duty to refer cases of suspected abuse to locally-established procedures.

It is not in the legal principles, but in the implementation of such partnership that much inter-agency discussion needs to occur. The tradition in youth work of recognising young women's rights and autonomy does not sit easily alongside the language of 'child protection'. Young women who are almost adults clearly have the ability and right to influence their own futures. It is useful, alongside recognising the general duty of child protection, to recall the important common-law Gillick principle: 'parental right yields to the child's right to make his own decisions when he reaches a sufficient understanding and intelligence to be capable of making up his own mind on the matter requiring decision'. This means that when girls have reached an age of sufficient understanding, they can be expected to participate in decision-making which affects their care.

The question of partnership between women attempting to develop feminist practice in different agencies is essential. Because the issue of violence will inevitably be present for any worker involved in informal education with girls and women, it is essential that workers are resourced and involved in inter-agency networks. Rape Crisis Centres and Women's Aid refuges are essential points of contact. There are now also a number of refuges which specialise in offering support to women from diverse Black communities. Members of the local social services departments are an essential point of reference and potential source of support. There has been a great deal of inter-professional fear and mistrust between community workers, social workers, teachers and health visitors.

The exercise of professional power in relation to young women who have experienced violence and abuse as children is fraught with difficulty, and has been defined as potentially the site of 'secondary abuse', compounding rather than counteracting the suffering that a young woman has already experienced (Driver and Droisen, 1989). There is a sense in which social work as a profession has been expected to carry the burden of intervention for a society which believes it right to protect children from exploitation and cruelty. The exercise of that authority can be done well or badly, in collaboration with the young woman or by ignoring her, in collaboration with other trusted adults and professionals, or in conflict and isolation. What is important is that feminists working in informal education in community settings do not isolate social workers as 'the enemy', thus potentially colluding with a persistent abuse of power in the name of retaining friendly relationships.

In the statutory power of social workers to intervene, there is clearly the potential for further abuse. It is also necessary to acknowledge that there is potential for alliance here, in a counter-power the law can exercise against the person perpetrating violence. In particular cases of child protection, where the working through of problems has not been possible on a co-operative basis, the police and the courts may have a part to play.

Young women who have a legal status as adults, through marriage, through having left the care system or having reached the age of 18, may also choose to involve the courts and the police to ensure their own safety in cases of rape and domestic violence. At this point, the advocacy and support role of the informal educator becomes very strong. Her own need for support, the opportunity for supervision and to explore her own practice cannot be stated strongly enough.

Finding a collective response

When women workers become deeply involved in particular cases, it is exhausting, partly because it seems too reactive, too involved in 'Band-Aid solutions', patching women up in order to send them deeper and deeper into a war not of their own making. However, the strength of a community-based response to young women's experience of violence lies in its recognition of the prevalence and normality of violence, while continuing to stress its unacceptability.

During the processes of informal education, it is possible for workers firstly to identify and explore the level of violence with which a particular group of young women is familiar, to explore what is and is not acceptable, and to help young women understand the nature of the violence against them. It is also possible for workers to affirm young women's capacities for survival.

In working with a group, it is very important that a worker shows that she is able to pick up cues, to instigate and build on conversations. It is through talking with a purpose that much of the valuable work of education occurs. Because so much of women's experience of violence has been made private and silenced, the process of finding a vocabulary and a name for what is happening becomes of the utmost importance. The case studies which follow all suggest ways, at a number of different levels, in which the process of naming and finding a voice can occur.

A young women's discussion and activity group

This is a daytime group, which has been meeting in a youth centre on an estate for about six weeks. The group is made up of young women who are all unemployed, and they are taking part in a programme of activities together and holding discussions about matters of importance to them, particularly health issues and employment issues. Ten young women attend the group, including one mixed-parentage Black woman. It is a mainly White estate.

After four weeks, one of the workers with the group notices that a particular young woman, Mary, is very subdued. She talks to Mary and finds out that she is upset. She has been told that the new baby she is expecting will automatically be very carefully monitored as a result of earlier non-accidental injuries to her first child. The worker checks this with her colleague from the 'patch' social services team, in confidence and with reference to the procedures, rather than the particular young woman involved.

The following week, Mary does not attend the group. The worker takes the opportunity to raise the question of what women expect from our relationships with men and what men expect from women, in a general way. One of the more vocal women in the group says very strongly that she never wants another man near her. Another woman mentions that perhaps Mary wouldn't want to come to the group looking a mess.

On the basis of this conversation, the worker suggests extending the programme to include some discussion of violence. Later, she becomes involved in the question of how increasing women's assertiveness in relationships can provoke a backlash from men. The group becomes a place where this 'backlash' is shared and coped with. Some silences have been challenged.

However, after the early weeks, the one Black woman who was attending the group stops coming. Much later, when the worker visits her, she finds out that it is because she has been told not to come by one of the other women in the group. Now the worker realises the need to find ways of breaking the silence about women not as coping with violence, but as perpetrators of it: in this case, of racist harassment. And she can make some connections about intimidation: the experience of intimidation by male partners, and the experience of intimidation by a white majority.

As so often, the themes of violence and harassment became part of the group work by inclusion of young women's experience. If the experience had not been voiced by the young women, would the worker have voiced it? Should the question of violence have been on the agenda from the beginning (Batsleer, 1986)?

In another young women's project in a mainly White, working-class area, the workers identified a young Sri Lankan woman living in great isolation with a very violent English husband. In this case, the workers' strategy was to support the creation of a group including other Asian women which she could attend. It is possible to move from identifying individual needs to establishing group processes in response (Green, 1995).

Putting violence on the group work agenda explicitly

Another approach is to include the issue of violence in group work from the very beginning, perhaps by including questions about the acceptability of violent behaviour in discussions about conditions for working well together. Many group workers start working with groups by establishing 'ground-rules' for work, and this often includes conditions which are understood and stated to be non-negotiable. Such conditions might include 'no discrimination', 'no personal attacks', 'no threats or intimidation'. Among many groups of girls who meet informally through community projects or youth centres, there are already well-established norms which run counter to these proposed groundrules.

Two part-time workers were working from a feminist perspective with a group of girls, both Black and White, who were members of a youth centre on an outer estate. They approached establishing a project with a group of girls by first of all paying attention to the issues that already existed among the girls.

One of the workers in particular was horrified by the level of aggression and bullying that existed among the girls, and it was apparent that there was a good deal of competition for boys among them. This was, to some extent, an economic competition, particularly in relation to who could get most for least on a Friday night, both in terms of having nothing to spend financially and of 'giving away' least sexually. The workers were clear that (hetero)sexuality and money were closely linked for the young women, that the competition and aggression among the girls were tied into the sexual/economic marketplace in which boys and girls related. The girls were also strongly anti-lesbian and attacked one of the workers as a lesbian.

On the basis of their observations, the workers decided to establish a programme of discussions based on the theme of resisting rape and sexual violence. The most aggressive girls in the group found this very hard to deal with, rehearsing the view that 'girls only get raped if they ask for it' very persistently and loudly. The workers struggled with a decision about whether the group was viable, either with or without the participation of the girls who were so vocal. In the end, the problem solved itself, as the most vocal girls stopped attending. The workers then set up a residential activity weekend for girls. Evaluations of the weekend record:

> I thought the idea of going in just a female group was better than a mixed group because we could relax more and the boys tend to mess about. (Hansford, 1993, p.9)

In her own reflections, the worker later observed that perhaps 'she had gone in at the deep end' in trying to work on the question of 'rape' from the beginning, and that she would be able to do this much more successfully now she had established relationships of confidence and trust with the girls, partly as a result of sharing a successful activity weekend with them (Hansford, 1993, p.9).

Successful group work on the theme of violence does seem to depend on workers having a clear agenda and an intention to break the silences and collusions about violence, while at the same time working at a pace that young women themselves can be at ease with.

Violence towards children as a problem for women's groups

Projects which attempt to establish non-violence as a basic method of working often struggle about how to respond to mothers' aggression towards their children. The Zion Community Health Centre in Hulme supports the Aisha childcaring group. The group offers an after-school club, playschemes and sessional creche care for a women's health drop-in scheme and a women's art class. The group also obtained funding to offer a holiday to 20 children from the area. They established a toy library and an accident prevention home loan scheme and supported the development of supported housing accommodation for young mothers in the redevelopment area of which they were a part.

In this context, project volunteers were able to develop training packages and policies to help them cope with issues such as difficult and challenging behaviour, as well as policies on assertive discipline and equal opportunities. It became possible for workers to hold discussions with mothers about the way they were treating their children, particularly in relation to smacking as a means of discipline, because the project was attending to young women's needs as a priority. In the context of a mainly Black (African-Caribbean) group, the issue of avoiding the brutalisation and criminalisation of another generation of young Black men is of great importance. Issues of how to de-escalate the level of violence which the whole community experiences are of great importance. Workers were able to relate discussions of childcare to the whole climate in which children are being raised (Zion Community Health and Resource Centre, 1993–4).

The Canklow Community Project in Rotherham, Yorkshire was established by a social services department and showed that a community-based approach to preventive work in childcare could be very successful in reducing the numbers of children on the 'at risk' register and 'in care' in a particular district:

> Better knowledge of networks and the general workings of the estate taught us more about certain families whose children had regular visits to hospital and were considered 'at risk'. The families were in fact under intense pressure with too many under-5s in the home, often with a single adult to supervise the children. Welfare rights information was instrumental in obtaining fireguards, safety gates, and where people were not entitled to these, voluntary groups were contacted for second hand items. Accessibility and the removing of worker/client barriers meant that vulnerable families came sooner with unpayable gas and electricity bills and Canklow's reputation as 'twilight city' was lessened as people did deals with the fuel suppliers on the telephone or agreed to let DHSS remove fuel payments at source. Previously some social workers had been called out in the middle of winter to unknown people with no gas or electricity, with all the resulting chaos. More than one family had been broken up by the need to receive children into care in such a situation, and rehabilitation where possible of these families was an early priority.
>
> Although our building is owned by the 'welfare', it was important to welcome parents feeling under pressure from childcare, and to help residents feel they had some control over the building. It was not always easy to dovetail this control with what management wanted from the building or the project: an onging balancing act was required; a stroll through a minefield may have been a better analogy at times. With women's groups and a general drop-in situation, coupled with liaison from other agencies on the best methods of intervention, the numbers in both categories – on the 'at risk register' and children in care – show a steady decrease and both have been firmly established in single figures for some three years. (Eastham, 1990, p.73)

The movement from 'victim' to 'survivor'

Workers in projects where young women are being supported after experiences of sexual violence – including projects in which young women have seen the offender punished by the judgment of a Court – have stressed the importance of group work linked to counselling as a method of developing self-help.

Young women need help in expressing anger, which often turns either inwards into self-harm and depression or outwards into aggression. Young women also need support in moving away from self-blame and to move from a 'victim' identity to a 'survivor' identity. The idea of being a 'survivor' is an important way of acknowledging that young women are still alive after having experienced life-threatening events. It acknowledges the seriousness of the suffering which many women have endured in the experience of sexual violence, and the ways that suffering is connected to killing, either in the form of the assaults suffered or in later despair, self-harm or attempted suicide. It also acknowledges the ordinary, everyday heroism of women who survive such threats. It can, however, become another obstacle if it seems to lock young women into an identity in which the experience of violence is the defining aspect of their lives (Nicholls, 1994).

Group work based in informal education can enable young women who are 'survivors' to survive by letting go and regaining a sense of everydayness in their lives.

A social support group for young women survivors of sexual violence which was established in Manchester at Forty Second Street, a resource for young people under stress, expressed the following aims in a publicity leaflet:

- to create a safe space for young women survivors of sexual violence, by validating their experience as young women and as survivors;
- to encourage mutual support and ownership of the group;
- to provide a mixture of structured and unstructured activities/discussion topics;
- to strive for a balance between social/fun activities, and opportunity for young women to talk about what's giving them a hard time .

Education programmes

The most important contribution that can be made by the work of community-based informal education is the development of education programmes which shift the emphasis away from victim-blaming by exploring myths and stereotypes and encouraging young women to define and assert for themselves what is and is not acceptable behaviour in relationships. The Zero Tolerance campaign has recently undertaken this work of political education very effectively through an advertising campaign. Community education workers linked to Rape Crisis projects and Women's Aid have developed programmes of education and training which are appropriate both for use with girls in school in the context of personal and social education classes, and for the training of workers in community projects. They explore the basis of myths and stereotypes about sexual violence, often by instigating discussion of statements which highlight those myths including:

- 'If a girl has agreed to sex before with a boy, she can't be raped.'
- 'A lot of women enjoy a fight/a beating. They look for rough men.'
- 'If you have an arranged marriage, you can't expect to consent to sex.'
- 'If you dress in a sexy way, you can't complain if boys bother you.'
- 'She can't have been raped, because she didn't resist.'
- 'Black men have a stronger sex drive than White men.'
- 'Black women ask for it more than White women because they are more physical.'

Workers then focus on exploring attitudes through discussion and enabling young women and young men to establish and understand a non-violent code of behaviour.

'Alternatives to Violence' workshops are also being established, to explore methods of resisting the escalation of conflict in communities, and these include workshops on resisting violence against women. However, all the education and consciousness-raising and support work which continues in relation to young women's experience of violence must be set in the context of a decline in material resources which can offer positive alternatives and which can strengthen women's position relative to that of men, emotionally but also economically. Clearly, there is a great deal to be gained from young women sharing strategies and ideas for survival. Apparently simple features of good practice – such as creating an atmosphere of enjoyment, offering peace and quiet and respite – are all part and parcel of a commitment to affirming young women's capacities for survival. But a safe haven is never going to be enough. Women's resistance to violence must be understood in the context of women's struggle against domination in all its forms.

Support for women workers

Facing up to the presence of violence in the lives of women very often means that women workers have to face up to the presence of violence in their own lives, sometimes for the first time, and understandings may be triggered as a result of events in a group. Sometimes, women are returned to the question of violence with a fresh perception and consciousness.

It is not good practice for any woman to work solely or exclusively on issues of violence. It is certainly not work that should be sustained indefinitely. Networks of women workers can help enormously in sustaining a feminist focus and analysis. They can provide encouragement and enjoyment and opportunities to relieve some of the stress created by the work. One of the main functions of women workers' groups is to organise this kind of support activity, and it needs to be regarded as a necessity, not a luxury. Networks of feminist workers can also provide an opportunity to establish more formal links of supervision for workers, and this is essential when workers are involved in work about violence, which can be extremely emotionally demanding. It can also be extremely exhilarating, and it is important that insights gained in the process of undertaking work in this area are shared.

Feminist support networks are sustained on the basis of a recognition of connection: connection between workers, and connections between workers and the young women who are part of the groups and projects. Claiming a 'professional' identity, claiming appropriate support and developing appropriate working methods are essential and are important method of avoiding the temptations to take on the sufferings of the world and become exhausted. It is very important that work against sexual violence is sustained and that workers are not exhausted. It is also important that the 'professional' identity does not become a barrier, a place of relative security, from which 'concern' is expressed, and not solidarity. To work as a feminist means to take the risk of acknowledging your connectedness with the violence women experience, and to develop strategies for work on that basis. In this way, 'creative support' may begin to create the conditions for change. Much of this work of support is about making it possible for certain stories to be told and heard, both by young women and by women workers.

Telling stories

Childhood stories of violence seem to incorporate other more up-to-date stories. At the moment, our culture seems fascinated with the violation of childhood. A feminist account of violence must give real importance to the words which young women themselves use to explain their experience. At any point, the experience of violence may not be the most significant aspect of a young woman's position. She may be more concerned to identify immediate issues that are affecting her than to recall earlier experiences of violence – especially at the point where contact with 'professionals' makes her most vulnerable, and where forgetting may be the most effective means of coping.

In that case, it is most appropriate for workers to respond to the 'here and now' demands of young women. These may be for safety on the streets if they are homeless; in relation to sex with clients if they are working as prostitutes; for basic support in relation to housing needs; in access to washing and laundry facilities, and even for warmth and shelter.

There may sometimes be a danger in the focus on sexual violence, particularly when it is linked to therapeutic accounts of healing the pain of the past, recovering past pain, healing and letting go. The danger lies in the tendency of this narrative to overwhelm all other accounts, including the specific accounts offered by young women. The professional, therapeutic voice then becomes the dominant voice, rather than simply being 'one account among others'. How does this happen? Firstly, there is a tendency – inherited from psycho-analysis – to look beyond the 'presenting problem' to a deeper structure. So, self-harm or homelessness or prostitution become the presenting problem – whereas the deep structure is a familiar pattern of male violence rooted in family forms. The account of this 'deep structure' seems more truthful than the 'surface' accounts of the present. Indeed, other accounts can then be presented as avoidances and resistances, coping strategies which may eventually fail unless the underlying problem is faced. This in-built ability to contain other accounts is very attractive to professionals, especially as it seems to offer a clear route for individual progress and change. The transition from 'victim' to 'survivor' comes to seem manageable, achievable within the power of a small group, or even within the power of an individual. Other accounts can seem more random, even provocative. Young women explain that they cut themselves up 'because they want to', that life is a game of 'survival of the fittest' and that bullies always win, or else they are living on the street because they are homeless, and they are homeless because they were evicted and have no money.

It is also possible that the focus on sexual violence is attractive for a certain form of feminist politics. It does allow a clear attention and a particular focus for demands for change. But such political clarity will not be successful alone. And it cannot be achieved by ignoring the voices of those it most desires to represent.

Sexual violence occurs in all communities, and the expectation that it will be more prevalent in Black communities is part of the racism which Black women have encountered when attempting to tackle the experience of violence on their own terms. Alliances between Black women's refuges and White feminist groups campaigning against sexual violence have sometimes been tense, especially when, for example, White feminist groups have overlooked the racism of housing allocation policies or the assumptions of social services departments in favour of apparently rather self-indulgent 'racism awareness training' (Mama, 1989).

However, the methods and principles explored in this chapter are the basis for work against violence against women in every community. When racial and sexual violence are inseparable – for example, in the context of racist attacks on Asian women within their homes – the process of making explicit and public the nature of the problem is still of primary importance.

Explicitly exposing the ideologies which support racial and sexual violence is a basic educational task. And the methods for supporting women who blame themselves or minimise the effect of such violence are rooted, whatever the context or the community, in an acceptance and belief that women are not to blame and are not to be blamed for the violence that is perpetrated against them.

9 Community, culture and identity

The words 'community', 'culture' and 'identity' are all difficult and compli-cated, capable of conveying in each case several meanings, which may be diametrically opposed. If each term is separately difficult, together they represent a nightmare for communication, so full are they of ideological resonance .

'Community', 'culture' and 'identity' are battlegrounds, and girls are at the centre of the skirmishing. They are each necessary words in the discussion of the practice of informal education and community development. I have explicitly chosen these words, rather than the alternative vocabulary of 'dis-course' and 'discursive practices', since they seem to me more suggestive of the link between language and meaning and the material world, without expressly privileging language. This chapter begins with an attempt to excavate some of their meanings and then focuses on current practice which explicitly addresses 'community', 'culture' and 'identity'.

Community

Like the word 'empowerment', to which it is connected, the word 'commu-nity' is like an aerosol spray, conveying an unlikely smell of sweetness to whatever phrase it is attached. It is rarely used with a negative connotation. Yet the ability of the word 'community' to connote an authoritarian form of social relationship, with a strong emphasis on duty and a lesser emphasis on individual autonomy and rights, is marked. In Britain, during the last fifteen years, there has been an an increasing sense of fragmentation and division. Margaret Thatcher, as Prime Minister, espoused a political creed which placed a strong emphasis on the benefits of competitive individualism. This was not a good period for 'community education'. Now the destructive nature of competitive individualism is increasingly being acknowledged.

Women, because of our role in the family, which has often been seen as the cornerstone of community, are once more looked to as bearers of community.

In the context of an increasing commitment to the values of community rather than the values of individualism, the understanding of appropriate opportunities for girls to develop will be framed within an understanding of shared community values. It seems likely that this is an improvement on competitive individualism, and that women will benefit when the values of mutual aid, association and co-operation are asserted. Yet this is by no means assured, and, as Elizabeth Frazer and Nicola Lacey have argued clearly in *The Politics of Community*, communitarianism, as it is currently expressed as a political theory, holds many dangers for women (Frazer and Lacey, 1994).

Community and the industrial working class

It is important to recall the association of the term 'community' with the history of the industrial working class and its inheritance. Current attempts to reclaim the word 'community' within Labour Party thinking may in part be testimony to this, and the association of the word 'community' with oppressed and exploited groups may reassert itself. Working-class culture, as it emerged in Britain, created community organisations – organisations such as the trade unions and the co-operative movement – which focused on meeting common rather than the individual needs through mutual aid.

There is certainly a moral value placed on 'community' and 'sociability', and it is seen as preferable to 'selfishness'. However, the basic reference point of 'community' is not morality. It is a sense of material necessity and a historical practice of organising within workplaces and within neighbourhoods to overcome, or at least to diminish, some of the difficulties of life in industrial and urban society.

As some of the forms of life, including particular workplaces and neighbourhoods – particularly those associated with heavy manufacturing industry – have disappeared, there has been a grieving and a sense of loss for earlier forms of working-class community (Williams, 1989; Seabrook, 1978). Alongside the grieving, there has been expressed, over and over again, a hope that women might, for the future, continue to develop and create new forms of community: often, it is recognised, despite rather than because of the active contribution of men (Seabrook, 1978; Campbell, 1993).

Bea Campbell's very moving account of the experiences of young people on some of the most poverty-stricken estates in Britain, *Goliath* (1993), suggests that there is a gender conflict occurring in communities which takes the form of a 'crisis of masculinity'. She depicts women as rooted in our responsibilities for kinship – for children and for older people – in relations of community support and community-building. When traditional sources of honour and self-respect for men are removed, she suggests, – particularly those associated with hard, waged work – it seems that only violence remains as a focus for masculinity.

The struggle which most dramatised that crisis for the white, industrial working class was the 1984–5 miner's strike. It is important to notice the essential role of women's organising in the long duration of that struggle, and the fact that, in many parts of the coalfields, it is the women's centres which were established in the aftermath of the dispute which are the strike's most enduring legacy. One of the women activists during the strike spoke of the work of the women's groups as the work of 'putting the bread on the table', and the phrase has stuck as an enduring description of women's work of community organising (Hyatt and Caulkins, 1992). Informal education work with girls and young women can contribute to a process of community-building.

Community and the life of 'ethnic minorities'

Girls and women are looked to at every level in society to create and sustain social bonds. But there is a danger that the term 'community' will come to have only a specialised reference to 'ethnic minority communities', as in the term, community relations council.'

Black communities in Britain are increasingly identified as bearers of a sense of community, of culture and identity, almost, it sometimes seems, on behalf of the majority and powerful society, where there is a lack of the qualities which these terms signify. There is a curious sense of envy generated within white society, as if the very cultural and community forms which have been created in the context of exploitation and oppression are not only a source of pride, but also a source of privilege in Black communities, which White society is denied access to.

It is important that youth and community workers acknowledge the sources of such community, and do not imagine that it is simply available for appropriation or copying in any setting. At the same time, second- and third-generation Black British young women have a great deal to teach about the ways new forms of community are developing: this will be explored later in this chapter.

Culture

'Culture' has been used to refer to 'the whole way of life and whole way of struggle' of a people. It points to the connection between the material and expressive, communicative dimensions of human life.

The rhetoric of multiculturalism

Floya Anthias and Nira Yuval Davis have pointed out that in the rhetoric of multiculturalism in education, people are seen as connected to a community through language. They suggest that the rhetoric of multiculturalism is based on 'community' (in contrast to the way that the rhetoric of anti-racism is based on colour) (Anthias and Davis, 1991). Much positive work that is undertaken with girls and young women draws on language, meaning and culture. It is involved in the recognition and creation of identities and histories.

The danger of a multicultural approach is that communities have been be defined in opposition and antagonism to one another, as if each were indeed an island. Each community has been seen as homogeneous and with clearly-identifiable and male community leaders. There was no attention to class or caste divisions within particular language communities, and no attention to the dominant culture and its forms of racism, or to the class divisions within the dominant culture. In other words, there is a danger that only minority and Black cultures will be named as 'communities' in this way, leaving the communities of the White majority unexamined and in a position of silent dominance.

In the most naive forms of multicultural education, culture is seen as homogeneous. But on any definition, 'culture' must be understood as moving, mixed, shifting, full of antagonisms and contradictions and new-ness, familiar oppositions and strange, unexpected mutualities.

No culture is fixed or homogeneous

Paul Gilroy has done more than any other writer in Britain recently to give an account of this context. In 'One Nation Under a Groove' (1993), Gilroy contrasts racist accounts of culture with the historical emergence of new cultures in the inner cities. In a discussion of cultural racism, he writes:

> Culture is conceived along ethnically absolute lines, not as something intrinsically fluid, changing, unstable and dynamic, but as a fixed property of social groups rather than a relational field in which they encounter one another and live out social, historical relationships. When culture is brought into contact with 'race' it is transformed into a pseudo-biological category of communal life. (Gilroy, 1993, p.24)

On the other hand, in the lived realities of post-war history:

> It is now impossible to speak coherently of Black culture in Britain in isolation from the culture of Britain as a whole. This is particularly true as far as leisure is concerned. Black expressive culture has decisively shaped youth culture, pop culture and the culture of city life in Britain's metropolitan

centres. The white working class has danced for forty years to its synco-pated rhythms. There is of course no contradiction between making use of black culture and loathing real live black people, yet the informal, long term processes through which different groups have negotiated each other have intermittently created a 'two-tone' sensibility which celebrates its hybrid origins and has provided a significant opposition to 'common-sense' racialism. (Gilroy, 1993, p.34)

Given the extent to which women are positioned as 'relationship-makers', it is not surprising that in the youth cultures of city life which Gilroy celebrates and defends, it is young women very often who are the bridge-builders, namers and source of connection. Informal education work with girls and young women from different communities needs to engage more and more with the creation and celebration of new hybrids of womanhood for the future.

Identity

In the work of community-building, racism is clearly both a powerful and destructive connection between different groups. When racism harnesses the term 'culture' in the way Paul Gilroy suggests – producing notions of self-contained and pseudo-biological groups – it also promotes concepts of 'identity' as relying on a recognition of sameness and an exclusion and definition of the 'other'. Identity can be built as a defensive/aggressive shield, to ward off 'the other' and to promote the recognition of the self-same. Building up the sense of community among the English residents of an area, for example, usually means building up a climate for racist attacks on people perceived as 'foreigners'. And this can be done without categories of 'race' or 'colour' ever being mentioned.

Community-building and the strengthening of identity can, however, be undertaken in a spirit of resistance to dominant definitions and out of a desire for affiliation and connection. So, in many parts of British cities, people from local neighbourhoods have rallied to shout: 'People of Hulme .... People of Newham ... People of Bolton ... have the right, here to stay, here to fight!' These have been the themes of anti-deportation campaigns in which people deemed 'illegals' by the government have been welcomed and sus-tained in particular neighbourhoods. Here, an identification with a particular neighbourhood has come to mean not a closing of ranks against outsiders, but a celebration of diversity and the principle of sanctuary.

Identity as a form of resistance

Patricia Hill Collins, writing in a North American context, expresses the importance of building up Black women's identity and community in the process of resistance to racism. She writes of the work of bloodmothers and 'othermothers' in extending and transmitting, both in their own families and in the family of the community, an Afrocentric world view. Hill Collins wrtes:

> The power of black women was the power to make culture, to transmit folkways, norms and customs, as well as to build shared ways of seeing the world that insured our survival [observes Sheila Radford Hill]. This power was neither economic nor political, nor did it translate into female dominance. This culture was a culture of resistance, essential to the struggle for group survival. (Hill Collins, 1991, p.147)

However, Hill Collins emphasises that in developing this power of Black women, Black feminist knowledge is rooted also in a recognition of a matrix of oppression:

> Dialogue is critical to the success of this epistemological approach, the type of dialogue long extant in the Afrocentric call-and-response tradition, whereby power dynamics are fluid, everyone has a voice, but everyone must listen and respond to other voices in order to remain in the community. Sharing a common cause fosters dialogue and encourages groups to transcend their differences. (Hill Collins, 1991, p.237)

In the British context, West Indian women whose families faced the brunt of racism in British organisations in the late 1940s and early 1950s were instrumental in establishing numerous voluntary and self-help organisations in the cities. These included Black churches, self-help projects on health, supplementary schools for children, and housing associations (Bryan et al., 1985). Similar initiatives have occurred within Bangladeshi and Pakistani communities, and there has been a strong, continuing connection with women and families 'at home' in Bangladesh and Pakistan, where conditions of poverty are different again. Sometimes, the channels for connection between communities are religious organisations and affiliations, which are then able to cross other kinds of belonging – even language, colour and nationality – in the name of faith. Aid to Bosnian Muslims and to Bosnian refugees is a good example of this kind of connection.

Attention to the building up of identity in the context of racism is a necessary strategy. In resisting racism, it is probably equally necessary to build up the networks, places and resources in which old identities can be transformed and possibly disappear.

Identity, culture and community as aspects of resistance to domination

As already noted, the critics of multicultural education have pointed out that attention to 'culture' and 'identity' is not sufficient to help children or adults understand or challenge racism. The phrase 'beyond saris, steel bands and somosas' has been used to indicate the necessity of developing educational strategies which promote community development and which challenge racism. It highlights the appropriation and fetishising of elements of culture and identity for the benefit of the powerful: the White Europeans who need to learn about 'difference'. When elements of a culture are fetishised and uprooted in this way, it destroys the recognition of culture as activity, of community as work. Difference becomes packaged into stereotypes, and these then prevent support services being developed which promote active participation. However, the attack on multiculturalism as an educational ideology shouldn't be used to dismiss the importance of some of the most basic needs a community has: for food, clothing and expression.

'Putting bread on the table' is work. The teaching of a mother-tongue – so basic to the constitution of culture and identity in any definition – is work. And it is women's work, whether the bread is chapati or rice or jam sandwiches, and whether the tongue is the English of the industrial North or the Punjabi of rural Pakistan or the Sylheti of Bangladesh. Despite the fact that the languages have very different status (as does the food), such shared activity may provide a basis of connection, just as Gilroy suggests the expressive culture of Black music can.

Culture, identity and community, when they are understood as aspects of resistance to domination, can be reclaimed as sources for challenging racism. Informal education with girls and young women has an important part to play in this process. In the rest of this chapter, I will look briefly at some of the 'false starts' that were made, and then point to a number of positive directions.

The problems of multiculturalism and 'race awareness' in youth and community work

It is now widely believed that the multicultural approaches and the development of 'race awareness training' which took place in youth and community work during the 1980s had a limited potential and effect, because they failed to address the needs of Black communities and at the same time did not take account of the power of the dominant culture.

White feminist projects were one of the places where the challenge of multiculturalism and 'race awareness' was most keenly embraced. The forms which the engagement took led all too often to 'guilt-tripping' and a consequent failure to develop strategies for change. As Sivanandan (1990, p.150) has noted, the guilt of the privileged is a useful mechanism for appearing to acknowledge injustice while retaining existing social relationships intact. It is useful to distinguish this from 'feeling ashamed' and the movement associated with shame – a judgement against one's own standards and a desire to see them reached.

This sense of guilt certainly did exist among white feminists in the 1980s, and when the philosophy of multiculturalism was combined with a particular form of 'identity politics', as it seemed to be in the equal opportunities strategies associated particularly with the Inner London Education Authority, a pattern of provision emerged which seemed to suggest that women could only work with girls out of a sense of shared identity. It was also suggested that the most powerful basis for work with girls was a commitment to developing culture and identity.

Clara Connolly's memorable account of these processes in 'Splintered Sisterhood' (1990) is a recognisable one, and she suggests that the emphasis on culture and identity in her project led to a failure to challenge girls (perhaps White girls in particular), a failure to build alliances against specific injustices, such as violence against girls and women or police attacks on given communities, and a failure to recognise the importance of cultural work which was forward-looking – such as the creation of Black British identities – rather than rooted in the (already-formed?) identities of adult workers (Connolly, 1990).

Not all multicultural work, even in London, shared these failings, and in some areas, the continuing alliances that were forged during the anti-racist movement of the 1970s have re-emerged in the 1990s, only a little shaken. Youth workers in the London Borough of Tower Hamlets who were instrumental in establishing some of the earliest girls' and young women's groups in the 1970s were still to be found active in the 1990s in organising women to oppose the British National Party candidate on the Isle of Dogs.

In cities where the communities which have attempted to build alliances are smaller, the issue has been as much one of lack of power, policy and resources to support initiatives such as Black resource centres and Black women's centres as it has been a failure of aims and purposes, which have clearly been focused in building coalitions across communities rather than in any form of cultural separatism.

In response to the failures of a multicultural agenda, there has been an attempt, within the field of youth and community work, to develop a Black perspective. The term 'Black' is understood to make reference to a political identity, forged out of resistance to imperialism, racism and White supremacy. (Various understandings of Black perspectives are found in the journal *Youth and Policy*, Summer 1995, which is devoted to the theme of 'Black Perspectives'.)

Optimistically, Black perspectives can be in alliance with non-racial/anti-racist perspectives which emerge from within White communities. The importance of the shift to Black perspectives is that it removes attention from the relationship between dominant and subordinate groups, rather in the way that separate and autonomous work with women removes the pressure of male dominance. It enables the work of building up intercultural alliances between Black communities to occur.

It is essential that the contribution of women to the development of Black perspectives is not marginalised, so the next part of this chapter considers some key contributions from Black women. It is also important – in the spirit of call-and-response – that the relationships between women from both Black and White communities continue to be explored, and it is with current practice in this area that the chapter ends.

The contribution of women to the development of Black perspectives

Nationality

A number of women have identified the re-emergence in the 1990s, of nationality and religion as a focus for community-building among Black British girls. Here, the new generation are seen as offering new perspectives to an older generation of educators. Although the term 'Black' is readily used as a shorthand, it is always qualified, often by reference to religion or nationality. 'Yemeni', 'Pakistani', 'Bangladeshi' are as useful as terms as 'Muslim' or 'Sikh'. These differences are recognised as differences, rather than necessarily mobilised as antagonisms within the alliance of 'Black'.

The issue of nationality and belonging is highly political, and it is also one in which the status of women as dependent on husbands or parents is clearly scrutinised. For example, the migration of young women from Pakistan, Bangladesh and India was made very difficult by the 'primary purpose rule', which made entry to Britain illegal if the primary purpose of migration was marriage (Lal and Wilson, 1986). The dual claim to a right to belong in Britain and to participate without discrimination in British society as an equal citizen, and also to claim affiliation and connection with one's history and family roots/routes, is necessary for girls who wish to claim both equality and autonomy. In the North-west, there is an active tradition of community work involvement in anti-deportation campaigning, and the place of young women in these campaigns, sometimes in support of other women who have used their homes as 'sanctuaries', is of great importance (Weller, 1987) .

Religion

Religious faith, and particularly the increasing significance of Islam in a number of different Black communities, is also seen as having been played down by earlier generations of community educators and as needing to be reasserted. Some women workers believe that a clear understanding of Islam from a woman-centred perspective will allow the bonds between different generations of women – particularly between mothers and daughters – to be expressed, renewed and developed, so that new possibilities can emerge for women now settled in Britain. There has also been some recollection of the part which Christianity played in the development of projects in Britain rooted in the West Indian communities.

Spiritual traditions are again proving themselves to be a resource of enormous importance. Each of the major religions offers an account of the significance and value of human life that can be set against the hostility and oppression which Black communities often face in White supremacist societies. The continued growth of the independent Black Churches with their roots in the Caribbean, the significance of Islam in a number of different Black communities, both African and Asian, the traditions of Sikhism and Hinduism – each offers a resource independent of the dominant European, Christian traditions. Religion also often poses a complex challenge to women, for the patriarchal nature and continuing male control of women is a major source of the power of the faith. Sakinna Dickinson, a youth and community worker in Tameside writes:

> Religion is an active force in all areas of life (within Asian communities anyway) and therefore it is necessary to enable discussion and debate to take place ... This is not the same as a religious practice group. Women can only shape an Islamic personal and social framework for themselves if they are clear about their own rights and responsibilities within that framework. (Dickinson, 1995)

A similar argument could certainly be made for women attempting to explore their relationship to other religious faiths.

It seems that the meanings of particular religious or cultural practices for women appear very different from 'inside' or 'outside' faith traditions. For example, the practice of wearing the *hijab* (veil), which has seemed so clearly a mark of female subordination to those outside the tradition, has become a mark of pride and self-respect for many Muslim young women. It is an assertion of individual allegiances and identity.

Particularly in relation to sexuality, religion can offer young women a way of marking a distance from the dominant commercialisation of female sexuality in capitalist societies. At the same time, all religions can produce a veil of ignorance and control of women (despite the recent apology by the Pope to all women), and what is appropriate for women is still defined by men rather than by women themselves.

Women educators working within the context of the 'appropriate', as defined by faith communities, often find themselves working at the boundaries of 'appropriateness'. There are questions about whether the women workers themselves are trustworthy, whether they can be accepted as sharing the faith even if they choose to express it differently, how they communicate a sense of respect for the older generation of women while enabling girls to make their own interpretations of the traditions the community offers. Workers find themselves needing to make clear delineations between a response to racism and issues which are issues of culture. For some women, the teachings on equality in the Koran offer a very clear basis for undertaking separate work with Muslim girls. Yet in practice, the development of Asian young women's groups, which now exist in many local authority areas, is a response to both. Such groups can organise events at times and with themes that are acceptable to parents.

There is an attempt to build a sense of 'women's space' across generations, in a society that has little understanding of the strength and resource of Asian women, and thereby to enable both young women and their own community to develop with pride. It is hoped that this will strengthen women in dealing both with conflicts with men within their own communities, and with the pathological view of Asian girls and women as passive victims, which is still the dominant view in British society.

The Asian Girls' Drama Project in Leeds has linked with youth workers to promote drama projects with Asian Young Women (Ashby, 1994):

> Asian girls' groups in Leeds at present offer a safe space for women to meet and talk and work confidentially. For some of the young women the group is one – and perhaps the only – place where they can voice their ideas and beliefs without fear of judgement ... Some issues young women have been keen to explore are racism, sexism, HIV/AIDS, arranged marriages, domestic violence, families and infanticide. Many of these issues are seen as taboo within Black (and white) communities. (Ashby, 1994, p.11)

The importance of the body

Skin colour emerges once more – and not at all surprisingly – as an experience to be talked about by young women. 'What do you mean, Black?' one young woman asked her community worker, 'Do you mean Black like me or Black like you?' – and in that conversation, the whole question of difference, heterogeneity and yet the importance of there 'being a mirror' in which Black girls can recognise themselves is revealed. To young women who want to talk about their experience of femininity being lived in their skins, to talk of Black as a political colour seems obvious in relation to the recognition of how racism operates, but it also seems to deny the reality of skin colour and its meanings in a racist society: 'Black is not a political choice; Black is what you are.'

The celebration of Black images of beauty has been a necessary working strategy in all Black young women's groups. The presence of a range of images of Black women is of the utmost importance. The absence of representation and the presence of racist representations, usually linked to a representation of sexual 'otherness' and availability, has been the focus of much important feminist writing which can form a resource for the development of practice (hooks, 1992).

Working across communities and cultures, and identifying diversity within communities

Projects which have worked with second- and third-generation Black British women from well-established communities often find themselves in a strong position to offer support to new migrants and to refugees. This is partly because the experience of migration is never far away, even in relatively settled communities, and also because such projects have a strong commitment to work which crosses boundaries and makes links between different communities.

Workers at the GAP Centre in Sheffield have worked as a 'racially'-mixed team from very early in the life of the project, working with West Indian, Pakistani and Yemeni working-class communities in Sheffield, as well as with White working-class girls. Recently, the established Somali community in Sheffield has grown as a result of the arrival of refugees from the war in Somalia. Not surprisingly, given their recent experiences, the daughters of the community are highly protected by their parents, but there was a recognition among the workers at the GAP project that this protectiveness was proving difficult for the girls, who sometimes reacted by taking very serious risks and seeming to show little regard for their own safety. GAP workers used funding available for crime prevention to establish a forum for the discussion of young women's safety. Together with young women from different communities, the workers established an agenda of themes in relation to 'risk' for young women, with a particular emphasis on the question of independence and the question of sexual harassment/exploitation. Young women then facilitated a conference, attended by teachers, police officers, health visitors and social workers, at which these themes were developed.

The GAP project workers' ability to work across communities and to build alliances across communities has also facilitated the development of a Black Women's Resource Centre in Sheffield.

There are many lessons for coalition-building in the experience of Black women workers. Jill Dennis, a worker at GAP, identifies a number of aspects to her work which have enabled her to make alliances. The first is the ability to continue to work and have links and connections at grass-roots level. Black women workers often continue to be very closely identified with the communities they are working in.

Secondly, the worker needs to be able to identify sources of funding and fight for them on behalf of a coalition of groups which are often excluded from the bidding process. In this way, a Black woman worker often experiences herself as the bridge who forges the coalition, stretched between marginalised communities and funding agencies, attempting to build up resources for young women. The experience of Black women often raises the question of 'on whose terms' alliances and coalitions are to be built. Black women have a great deal of experience of slowing down processes of agenda-setting that are taking place in White funding bodies in order to create a forum for Black as well as White voices to be heard.

Thirdly, the experience of building alliances between different Black communities is not based on an abstract principle of 'the need to build alliances', but on very specific and possibly narrow shared concerns – such as the need for safety and protection, and the parent–daughter issues this raises. It is also based on a recognition of important, shared experiences of migration and settlement, and of the hostilities of racism. Similarities of experience can be glimpsed and a connection can be made, first in imagination and then in reality.

The forms taken by cross-cultural alliances clearly depend on the power relationships at stake. It may be easier to build alliances among girls from a number of different marginalised communities than to cross barriers where major political power is at stake. Here, the experience of girls' work in Northern Ireland is very instructive: 'cross-community projects' have tended to be dominated by boys, and yet girls have also experienced the restrictions of living in a divided society, particularly the restrictions on mobility. Once cross-community projects from a local youth centre were established, it clearly became much easier for girls to visit and make contact than it was for boys.

The report on equality of opportunity for the Northern Ireland Association of Youth Clubs (Trimbell, 1990) points out that the sense that 'it's different for girls' has both positive and negative aspects. It is harder for young men to make visits to areas of 'the opposite religion' because of the expectation that they will be aggressive. However, the pressures on young women not to form relationships across the divide are very strong, and a young woman

who does so is strongly censured by her own community. Again, the importance of having a focus for connection which is separate from the fact of connection is very strong.

Youth work with Black young women is also enabling the experience of
diversity within communities to be explored. In 'Making Youth Work
Accessible to Black Women in the North East of England', Yasmin Kutub
(1995) writes about the benefits which arose from the establishment of a
specific training course for Black women:

> During the first session, some of the students began to talk about their own
> experiences of racism, which ranged from institutional forms, in relation
> to employment (or the lack of it), housing and education, to more insidi-
> ous forms such as harassment on the streets, vandalism of homes and
> cars and even some asssaults ... For some it felt like the first time they
> had been able to do this in a supportive environment, and others felt
> they had been denied this opportunity on other courses. (Kutub, 1995,
> p.88)

Yasmin Kutub goes on to explain how the course facilitated the exploration
of diversity:

> Usually, in relation to equal opportunity issues, there is an expectation
> that Black women will only be concerned with responding to issues of race
> and gender. However, one of the main focuses of the course was to
> acknowledge the diversity that exists within Black women, and to shatter
> the myth (which is often internalised by us) that we are one homogeneous
> group. By examining other forms of oppression, and drawing analogies
> with the students' own experiences of oppression via racism and sexism,
> we gave students the opportunity to explore issues such as lesbianism
> within the Black communities, and class issues as they affect Black people.
> (Kutub, 1995, p.88)

It is interesting that for many projects rooted in Black communities, and for
work with girls in Northern Ireland, it has been international work which has
offered a vehicle for continuing to build connections.

Internationalism

In many cities, the celebration of International Women's Day has become a
focus for the work of women's projects and young women's groups.
International Women's Day on 8 March became a focus for women's politics
in the early years of the twentieth century and was first commemorated to
mark the beginning of a strike of garment workers, who were demanding

equal pay. The celebration of International Women's Day was revived in the 1960s and became a focus for demonstrations on subjects such as equal pay and childcare.

In the 1980s and for the girls' work movement, an increasingly cultural focus for the work was developed, and to some extent there was a decline in the political and international focus. This has been revived in projects which work across different communities, particularly by Black workers. In such projects, although International Women's Day remains a focus for celebrating women's friendships and for offering non-traditional opportunities to young women, there is also the dimension of informing and educating ourselves about women's struggles internationally. The events might include drama, dance, fashion shows and sharing food. They also include a celebration of the success and achievements of women, and celebrities are often invited.

Other methods of sharing information and promoting education include showing films and videos, organising bookstalls and inviting speakers, followed by a discussion. In some cities, the overseas student community offers a point of connection, and where there are shared interests in development, projects such as Southern Voices, which aims to link the experience of people from the South with the work of development agencies based in the North, can offer inspiration.

International work can also take young women's projects beyond a narrowly European focus in the opportunities for international exchange work. A number of projects have used the Commonwealth Institute to facilitate visits and exchanges with commonwealth countries. International work can explore cultural forms such as writing, film and video to explore how women are dealing with the issues of rights and responsibilities 'back home'.

Call and response: Can White women listen?

If it is true to say that questions of material survival – 'putting bread on the table' – and questions of communication – 'teaching the mother tongue' – are constructed as women's work, then it may be that connections between Black women's projects and community organisations run by White working-class women will be effectively based on questions of economics and questions of communications.

In West Yorkshire, the Low Pay Unit has provided a forum for meetings between women workers in the textile industry internationally. Castleford Women's Centre, which arose from the work of a miners' wives' support group during the miner's strike of 1984–5, has focused both on opportunities for employment for women and on the development of educational opportunities. The connections between women in different centres in West

Yorkshire are potentially strong, and young women across communities need resourcing and encouraging to make those connections.

One of the strongest political alliances of the last decade – although an unsuccessful one at the time – was that between miners' organisations and the inner-city Black communities, and much of this alliance-building was facilitated by women. Paul Gilroy noted:

> During that industrial dispute, highly dissimilar groups were able to connect their fates across the divisions of 'race', ethnicity, region and language. For a brief period, inner city populations and the vanguard of the orthodox industrial proletariat shrank the world to the size of their immediate communities and began, in concert, to act politically on that basis. In doing so, they supplied a preliminary but nonetheless concrete answer to the decisive political questions of our age: how do we act locally and yet think globally? How do we connect the local and immediate across the earthworks erected by the division of labour? (Gilroy, 1993, p.46)

When women's work of community-building in White working-class communities is undertaken in a spirit of resistance and struggle, it is much more evident how the traditional narrownesses and chauvinisms associated with Englishness in some working-class communities can be broken down. Where White women workers see analysis of and resistance to racism as necessary to feminist politics, rather than as a diversion, alliances can more readily be built. Some White feminists have undertaken joint work with Black workers, male and female, to offer educational programmes about racism in predominantly White communities, and to offer support and development opportunities to Black young people, who are often intensely isolated in such areas (Green, 1995).

The most concrete basis for alliance and solidarity seems to be where there are survival issues at stake, where the social existence of groups is in jeopardy. It is also likely that women will be among those most strongly insisting on alliance. Within that context, there is a real need to ensure that the question of the autonomy of women, perhaps especially young women, and women's need to develop their own goals are not lost.

In order to avoid the clear danger of community being established on the basis of the subordination of women's own potentials and goals, perhaps the surest basis for alliance between Black women and White women of diverse communities is mutual pleasure and enjoyment. It is to the unexpected friendships between girls and young women in the 'hybrid cultures' of our cities that feminist education with girls and young women should look, in anticipation of receiving an accurate, informal education.

10 Established patterns, new directions: The organisational context of work with girls and young women

Although the places in which informal education work with girls and young women occurs do change, and there have been marked shifts as a consequence of the Conservative restructuring of local education authorities, it is important to begin by recognising the role of a tiny department within most LEAs known as 'The Youth Service'. The work of youth services developed in partnership with voluntary organisations such as the Young Women's Christian Association and the Girls' Friendly Society, which have the promotion of the welfare of girls and young women as a major aim. There has been a connected partnership with the uniformed voluntary organisations, such as the Guides and other faith-based organisations.

Since 1945, youth services and other voluntary organisations have offered an apparently open space in which social educational work with young people can be developed. This has seemed to be in contrast with the more explicitly regulated areas of work, such as social work (where issues of child protection are among the statutory responsibilities held by workers) or the probation service (regulated directly by the criminal justice system) or schooling (regulated by the demands of the National Curriculum and the examination system).

From the beginning of the establishment of professional training courses in the field of youth and community work, the literature has stressed the 'voluntary principle' and 'the principle of association', and there has been a stress on participation, alongside a developing understanding of the aims and purposes of social education and advocacy. However, as a number of writers have pointed out, the absence of statutory control does not mean the absence of regulation. There are now a number of analyses of the regulation of girls and of women workers by the informal domination of boys and men and by the dominance of the 'male agenda' (Sawbridge and Spence, 1991). But wherever there is domination, there is also resistance, and it was the combination of the explicit commitments of 'youth service' organisations with their failure to respond to the needs of girls and young women from different communities which opened up the space for feminist and woman-centred practice from the 1970s onwards.

Youth service-based work included important initiatives from national and regional organisations (such as the Girls' Work Unit of the National Organisation of Youth Clubs) and local projects and events.

Patterns of separate provision

'Separate provision' for autonomous work with girls occurs in different settings and has been made available in a number of different ways. In some local authorities, girls' clubs and young women's activity groups are given their own time slots within the context of mixed clubs and projects. This is usually determined by the male-dominated patterns of the mixed projects, rather than any consideration of the needs or expectations of young women – in more than one Northern city, all the girls' nights have run to coincide with the weekday evening when local football matches are played.

In another pattern, women workers are nominated to undertake 'separate work with girls' in the context of busy, mixed club sessions. This is really an impossible pattern of tokenism, which should be avoided at all costs. Fair and equal treatment of boys and girls is important in mixed sessions, and working out strategies to promote this way of working is the responsibility of all staff. This may well form a complementary strategy to promote separate and autonomous work, but one should not be used to substitute for the other.

Another pattern is to establish separate young women's centres. These have sometimes been city-centre-based or borough/city-wide resource centres and meeting places. In other cases, young women's centres are to be found in flats or houses on council housing estates. Another pattern is to allocate a set of rooms within a larger building.

'Separate provision' encompasses outreach projects and detached work, and such projects usually focus on the needs of young women who are perceived to be particularly 'marginal' or 'vulnerable'. The information, support and advocacy aspects of social education practice can be seen at their strongest in such work, which includes work with homeless young women, work with disabled young women who have been segregated from 'mainstream' provision, and work with young women who are working as prostitutes. A great deal of the innovation associated with detached youth work and outreach work has been found in the voluntary sector – both in the 'old' voluntary sector, with its roots in nineteenth-century philanthropy, and the new voluntary sector with its roots in the 'New Left' community politics of the post-1968 generation. However, even in the apparently radical approach of detached work, male perspectives have still dominated. The model of street-based work was challenged by women workers who pointed out that:

1 Young women tend to have more domestic commitments and tasks than young men.
2 Parental pressure to be at home is exercised more with young women than young men.
3 Women are more vulnerable on the steets than men, especially at night. (Youth Work Unit, 1983, p.4)

Women workers, such as those who created the document *Looking Beyond Street Level* from which this statement comes, transformed the understanding of detached work. Within the practice of feminist work with girls, detached work and outreach work can be understood as an essential aspect of all informal education, which must constantly be returned to and which links to group-building and to the development of projects and organisations in a spiral of working methods, rather than as a completely separate form of work.

The links between feminist approaches and the detached youth work traditions of working with young people on their own terms and on their own agendas in their own places are strong. But when young people's own places are the bedroom rather than the streets, as is often the case with girls, new insights about 'starting where young people are' have to be developed. The challenge of creating girl-friendly spaces where society provides none has to be accepted, and this is a collaborative activity between girls and young women and women youth workers. It cannot be undertaken solely 'on young women's own terms'.

Older organisations, such as the YWCA, the Guides and the Girls' Friendly Society, have sometimes been willing to support new work, and there are links – personal, professional and political – between work in the voluntary-sector youth organisations and the new 'feminist voluntary sector', which includes Women's Aid, Rape Crisis Centres, Lesbian Line and projects responding to the needs of survivors of sexual abuse. A good example of this kind of coalition in the voluntary sector is the work being undertaken by Manchester Survivors' Project, which draws on feminist insights, the strengths of trained social workers , counsellors and youth and community workers and the resources of a partnership between the local authority and the Richmond Fellowship, an established voluntary organisation in the mental health field.

It will be apparent that these patterns of provision, which have their roots in the youth service, are not exclusive to it. There are an increasing number of partnership projects – with health authorities drawing on critical support for the 'Health of the Nation' agenda, with the probation service drawing on the 'crime prevention' agenda, with residential social work and child care agencies drawing on the child protection agenda. Skills, practices and principles developed in the crucible of youth work are very much necessary in the development of new partnerships. Health authorities establishing young women's health centres, social work teams looking for ways of offering support to young mothers, counsellors considering different methods of support to survivors of abuse, schools looking for ways to encourage and enable young women from a variety of backgrounds and communities to develop their potential are all now drawing on the principles of informal education with young women and girls.

Work with Asian girls has been represented as 'other'

A division between work with girls (usually meaning work with White girls and African-Caribbean girls) and work with Asian girls has existed from the very beginning. From an anti-racist perspective, it is clear that White feminists have sometimes been able to open up or prevent the allocation of resources to Black women's groups. Although White feminist work originates in a resistance to the malestream, it can occupy a remarkably strong 'gatekeeping' role – able to influence the policy and sometimes resourcing in key areas, and able to deny access to Black women's groups or promote participation of Black women's groups in wider forums. These inequalities in access to the power structures make alliance-building a very difficult process.

A great deal of the work in Black women's projects has drawn on voluntary initiatives from within the communities themselves, from the grassroots level – organisations such as the Palace Youth Project in Leeds and Abasindi in Manchester provide supplementary education from an African perspective for children who have their histories and experiences denied in the curriculum of White schools. Similarly, within Bangladeshi and Pakistani communities, much informal education work builds on already-existing women's networks. However, there is often an absence of connection between women's groups based in different communities, which can only be attributed to the workings out of racism within service provision. Black women workers consistently report a sense that their work is dismissed, ignored or simply not valued. The working party which reported to the DES on girls' work in 1989 had the following comments to make:

> In some cases, especially in voluntary organisations, work with young Black women is exciting, positive and evidently meeting their needs; it is purposefully separate and autonomous. In other cases however the existence of separate groups amounted to their having been virtually abandoned by the Youth Service management. One group of 27 Asian girls had never been visited by a Youth Officer. (DES, WO and NACYS, 1989, p.12)

Particularly in relation to work with Asian girls, where convenient and destructive myths about the complete 'otherness' of language and culture still prevail, separate provision can become a vehicle for sustaining the fear and ignorance of a racist culture as much as a positive basis for work. So the pioneering cross-cultural work which occurs in many projects is never acknowledged, valued and learned from at the level of management structures, and workers are denied appropriate support to develop purposeful, autonomous work. This lack of support is a danger throughout the field in relation to work with girls. When this is combined with racism, it makes it far too easy for the work to be undermined and discredited, and individual women workers can carry a very heavy burden.

Some local authorities developed positive action projects in which Black women found themselves promoted as a result of the 'two for the price of one' syndrome – a rather cynical phrase which encapsulates the perception that may be held by the women themselves or by people around them, that they were promoted because they were Black and because they were women. Very often, they have found themselves unsupported and expected to deliver, usually on the back of a postage stamp, a whole range of informal education provision to communities whose needs are neither recognised nor acknowledged within White structures. Language and support work – in the form of posts within education authorities, and in posts in social services and health authorities – has been a major area of work for women workers from Asian communities.

Again, it seems to be in the area of detached and outreach work that some of the most woman-centred work has been able to take place. It seems that Black women have worked creatively with the 'crumbs' dropped in the form of positive action strategies from the 'White man's table'. Projects focusing on Black women's health needs, on relationship issues, on ways of resisting racism and providing advice on immigration and nationality, mother-tongue projects and welfare projects, and Black women's refuges have all emerged, as well as young women's projects which offer the opportunity to young women to build up their own strong positive identity.

Perhaps as will always be the case among the most oppressed communities, the basic questions of welfare and the questions of education development combine.

The argument for separate and autonomous work with girls has been well established, but it is clear that the contexts in which such work can occur have changed and will continue to change.

The importance of partnership in provision

It is clear, too, that informal education work will no longer be only youth service-based, but will occur in a number of different settings, particularly perhaps in the voluntary sector and in the partnership provision which is being encouraged by patterns of funding based on contracts for specific services. The authors of *The Youth Work Curriculum* (Newman and Ingram, 1989) identified a range of organisations in contact with youth workers. These included community organisations such as sports clubs, religious organisations, Rotary Clubs and trades councils; educational agencies such as schools, the careers service, basic education, adult education, training agencies, further education colleges and outdoor education centres; local government departments, and caring agencies such as probation, social services, intermediate treatment, health departments, substance abuse agencies, family planning, Relate, Shelter and St John Ambulance. The authors of this document include 'race relations' and 'Equal Opportunities Commission' under caring organisations. The kinds of contact that might exist between youth workers and such a range of organisations would range from referral of young people to other services, to partnership projects and joint working.

Given that most of these organisations are male-dominated or have a male-dominated agenda, it is likely that the partnerships which will emerge in this context will once more prioritise boys, and that issues concerning a wide range of different groups of girls and young women will be pushed to the edge unless there is a clearly-articulated strategy to counter this process.

There is therefore a need to explore a number of different aspects of 'difference' and to consider ways of rebuilding alliances or making them anew in the competitive marketplace in which organisations supporting girls' work now exist.

There is also a need to consider the ways in which older commitments and methods can be renewed with the next generation of young women. The issue of how work is shared across generations is very important. Linked to this are questions of the definition of youth with which this book has been, in part, preoccupied. In relation to a long-standing discourse concerned with 'risk' and 'protection', young women are again being infantilised and seen as children. The question of how to sustain a critique of this discourse while retaining resources and funding is very important. What kind of national and international forums are necessary to sustain a feminist approach to informal education with girls and young women is also a critical question.

Association across diversity, not problems as false unities

There is a need to recognise and acknowledge the plurality of focuses for autonomous work with girls and young women. It is by now clear that there is no automatic focus of unity in seeking to build solidarity among women. It is also clear that although 'youthfulness' as a social construction does render girls vulnerable and position them in similar ways – in ways distinct from say middle-aged and old women – being young is not, on its own, a basis for connection. How does a young woman whose primary focus of attention is the need to leave an oppressive family connect with a girl of a similar age who is going to have a baby and needs the support of her mother? Is there the possibility of discussion between a young woman who wants to be heterosexually active and needs support in obtaining and using appropriate contraception, another who finds herself in love with her best friend and another who is planning to marry someone approved of by her parents. It is now absolutely necessary to recognise that the basis on which workers promote association among young women will not be simply, if it can be at all, on the basis of shared assumptions about what it means to be a woman.

In some areas and in some projects, it is possible to make the development of association across diversity a very explicit aim. At other times, the arguments for and the promotion of separate and autonomous work are likely to be couched in terms of young women's experience of risk or young women as problematic. Such definitions produce false unities which project workers then have to work very hard to undo.

These processes of definition are closely associated with the institutional and organisational location of practice. Histories of professional definition cut across attempts to state shared political values and aims. Funding of projects sets aims and purposes for work which are not easily discounted. So a major question which currently confronts practice is about the kind of institutional and organisational settings that are re-emerging which will allow the work to continue. A number of new frameworks and coalitions seem to be emerging, including an alliance between workers in play work, adult education and community development. There are also new proposals for the accreditation and validation of community work professionals, linked to the project of community care. The impact of curriculum changes and the development of the National Curriculum in formal schooling means that there is now a clear place for the role and work of informal educators in promoting person-centred educational processes in schools.

Informal education, of the kind this book describes, will increasingly struggle for space in places where the agenda of education and development work is already very heavily directed from elsewhere. One of the major tasks of youth and community workers will be to define their work in relation to a multidisciplinary team and to continue to assert, within projects which may well have a very different focus, the need for autonomous work which proceeds from agendas set by young women themselves.

These are all essentially organisational questions, so in the rest of this final chapter, I will indicate the debates that have emerged in the 1990s which point to a direction for the future.

Difference and alliance between professionals

New patterns of funding through partnership arrangements are requiring new kinds of interdisciplinary networks and cross-professional working. It will become increasingly common for women trained in informal education as youth workers and community workers to be working as members of staff teams alongside counsellors, social workers, teachers, midwives and health visitors. The challenge for feminist practice is to be able to cross these disciplinary boundaries and work in ways which promote the recognition of the rights and potential of young women. Much of the current experience of interdisciplinary working tends to be in areas where young women's behaviour has been defined as risky or problematic. Feminist practice in informal education, which is taking place in the context of a multidisciplinary team, therefore has to negotiate both the demands of interdisciplinary working and the formulation of an agenda for work which is not problem-centred.

An interesting example on interdisciplinary working can be found in the pupil support services, for children who experience emotional and behavioural difficulties. The Peacock Centre in Manchester has adopted an innovative approach to work in this area, and from the beginning has offered both separate and autonomous work with girls, in groups and individually. The Peacock Centre employs both teachers and youth workers, and works with clinical psychologists and social workers in making an assessment of young women's needs. The psychological services do not have a method of assessing young women's needs which might focus on the gender issues involved, and while many of the young women involved in the Peacock Centre may have experienced sexual abuse, the impetus to establish separate girls' groups came from the teaching and youth work staff associated with the centre.

In relation to working with young women who are escaping abusive relationships, the teachers and youth workers in the pupil support team had to work hard to establish their credibility to work in this area, particularly with social workers, who had themselves undertaken a specific training and possessed a specific expertise. It was both the commitment of the educators and the willingness of the social workers to set aside assumptions about expertise which allowed the shared work to develop. The fact that the city council had adopted a policy for women which itself promoted interdisciplinary working also helped. Key members of the group which developed the work on child protection had met as members of a domestic violence working party. In this way, organisational structures and policy commitments at the level of the city council enabled women workers from different professional backgrounds with a history of mutual suspicion to recognised shared values and develop effective working relationships.

The fact that the pupil support services straddle the social work/education divide also makes it possible for work with girls which is rooted in the assessment of risk – still, all too often, associated with 'promiscuity' – to take on a role which, through educational work, challenges the conditions which create the difficulties. Work can focus on the transition from primary to secondary school, a transition in which the assertiveness and self-esteem of girls can take a severe knocking. Within the curriculum of personal and social education, teachers from the pupil support services have promoted the idea of 'a child protection curriculum'. This enables the establishment of girls' groups which work on assertiveness, developing ways of talking about feelings and emotions, the place of secrets in our lives, and the relationship between trust and touch. Within the National Curriculum for schools, it has proved possible to incorporate the aims of 'the child protection curriculum' within the targets for attainment in speaking and listening, for example.

It is interesting that the staff involved in the Peacock Centre who trained initially as teachers come from subject backgrounds which are often seen as marginal to the school curriculum: from PE and domestic science, for example. Perhaps these disciplines lend themselves to the building of relationships and co-operative working which are identified as essential to interdisciplinary team-building. All the women involved in the pupil support services identify themselves as strong women and as offering potential role models to young women, though not all would use the word 'feminist' to describe themselves. There is a strongly-female organisational culture, and work with girls has strong support from the management group. This, in its turn, gives both youth workers and teachers the confidence to work alongside social workers and clinical psychologists, while retaining a sense of expertise.

Other examples of projects which have successfully established alliances across professional boundaries can be found in the voluntary sector, where partnership funding and the development of contracts for the provision of specific services have led to the creation of new forums for interprofessional discussion. At Forty Second Street in Manchester (a community-based resource for young people under stress), projects have drawn on funding from the health authority, the Mental Health Foundation and from local authority joint funding (which includes a contribution from the social services department). There has been little input of funding from education-based sources. The project draws explicitly on an agenda which is concerned with empowerment in relation to the mental health system and employs workers from a number of different backgrounds to staff its projects. The fact that staff may identify as feminists and share a similar political agenda for the empowerment of women in relation to the mental health system does not mean, for example, that the tensions between a counselling-based approach to work with young women under stress and a community action-based approach will disappear.

These interprofessional alliances are creative and necessary and may offer the only resource base for some time to come. Partnership funding has also extended to work with the police force and work with the probation service, for example in addressing issues of young women's safety. At the same time, it is very apparent that the perspectives of informal education will be quite marginal within interprofessional alliances, because it comes with no money, as the poor relation to most projects. It is important that a separate organisational and funding base is retained for informal education/community education (a case that has long been argued for the youth service by writers concerned with youth work – for example, Davies, 1986).

It is also absolutely necessary when professional partnerships are entered into that there is clarity about the aims, curriculum and methods of informal education, and the distinctive emphasis which feminist youth workers and community workers can bring to a coalition. In the absence of a great deal of financial power, the power of clarity of purpose and commitment to certain aspects of practice will have to be drawn on.

Interprofessional alliances are sometimes envisaged at a 'high-level strategy' meeting. For example, prior to the recent merger of the two departments, there were consultations between the Department of Employment and the Department for Education about the form of training for work in the fields of informal education and community care. Feminist agendas have occasionally had a voice at national level in the civil service. More recently, a Department for Education working party published a report on *Youth Work with Girls and Young Women* (DES, WO and NACYS, 1989). Its recommendations were as follows:

1   Voluntary organisations concerned with provisions for girls and young women and local authorities should formulate a policy for youth service provision and make girls' work central to this policy.
2   Providers of the youth service should develop an action programme for the development of work with girls and young women.
3   Alongside recommendations 1 and 2, an analysis should be made of the allocation of financial resources for youth work, to identify comparative amounts spent on work from which young women directly benefit, and to set financial targets to redress any imbalance.
4   A fresh look should be taken at meeting accommodation needs, to secure more appropriate premises for the development of the work.
5   Voluntary organisations and local authorities should additionally show how they have addressed and are meeting the needs of specific groups of young women.
6   Positive action should be taken to increase the number and seniority of women in the youth service.

7   A review of access to training courses should take place to ensure that women are not disadvantaged.
8   A unit or units should be set up for the development of girls' work nationally.

The National Youth Agency which acts on behalf of the government in co-ordinating youth work-based initiatives, has a governing body elected by a number of different constituencies. One of the constituencies is the women and girls' organisations, which includes representation of the Guides and Girls' Friendly Society. The demise of the National Organisation for Work with Girls and Young Women has left a significant gap where autonomous work with girls from a feminist perspective was represented at the level of the National Youth Agency. If the recommendations of the DfE working party were implemented, this would allow a new national organisation to develop and have a voice within national and international forums.

At a regional and metropolitan level, local authorities can still provide a forum for feminists to make alliances across professional disciplines within the Welfare State. Such alliances can be facilitated by senior managers and by elected councillors. They may take the form of consultation forums and working parties – such as the successful domestic violence working parties which have been established by chief executives' departments in a number of councils, or curriculum development groups within education authorities. It is in these apparently unpromising places that networking may occur which can achieve shifts of resource and emphasis in the direction of empowering work with young women. The presence of some women at middle-management level in organisations is certainly essential to the development of these forums. Women managers – especially those with their roots in community-based initiatives or who have made explicit feminist commitments – need to be regarded as allies and actively supported and encouraged to facilitate the development of feminist practice.

Alliance across difference: The different voluntary sectors and the contract culture

Cutting across the difficulties and possibilities of partnerships between professionals is the problem of the poisonous meeting between a Thatcherite project of privatisation and the introduction of market principles into the provision of education and welfare services on the one hand and the fragmentation of the 'new social movements' on the other. Many of the projects – including the girls' work projects with which this book is concerned – which came to form the 'new voluntary sector' during the 1970s are founded in the self-help principles and resistance to State control associated with both a libertarian left agenda and with liberal community politics.

The 1980s saw a convergence between the agenda of the government and the ideology of much of the 'new voluntary sector' in a resistance to State control. Resourcing now happens through a quasi-market-based system of achieving contracts for particular aspects of service provision. This is thought to make service provision more efficient and able to remain closer to the agendas of service users/clients/customers.

However, the hidden hand of the market seems as unlikely as it has always done to distribute its largesse equally. Somehow, even with the freedom and the creativity of the market at work, established hierarchies re-establish themselves. Services geared to the needs of boys are more easily funded. Provision for girls all too readily becomes provision for girls who already have access to resources: young women's projects which have never had a voice or representation in funding bodies struggle to establish a presence at all in the funding game. Competition for resources favours those who already have access to resources, and even among the habitual losers there is a scramble for advantage which can easily destroy earlier attempts at coalitions.

The inheritance of 'identity politics'

If one side of the difficulties which are facing girls' work comes from the divisiveness and competitiveness of the contract culture, the other comes from the problems of 'identity politics' created in the forums of equal opportunities strategies in the 1980s. The impact of a liberal equal opportunities agenda has now been carefully explored and subjected to critique (for example, Baker, 1987).

In the context of declining resources, the potential for groupings based on apparently exclusive identities to compete with one another for the crumbs has been intense. There has been a tendency in this context for a feminist agenda or a 'women's agenda' to be perceived as a White agenda (with the diverse needs of women from different Black communities subsumed under a 'race' agenda), or to be perceived as a heterosexual agenda (with the needs of lesbians and bisexual women subsumed in a 'gay' or 'queer' agenda). Further, the needs of women as mothers and carers seem to have been most actively addressed as part of a 'children's agenda', leaving the women's agenda for those who do not have children.

In the context of identity politics, the women's agenda becomes a disappearing space. There is a lack. It is in part as a result of these pressures that the National Organisation for Work with Girls and Young Women has disappeared and will have to be created again in a new form which recognises the diversity and complexity of organising as women.

In this context, it is vital that any organisation of women is anti-separatist in its orientation and prepared to ally, for example, with the National Organisation of Lesbian and Gay Workers, the National Organisation of Disabled Youth and Community Workers, the National Black Workers' Conference and with Sia, the National Development Agency for the Black Voluntary Sector. Networks of projects based in poor communities – such as the Outer Estates Network funded by Church Action on Poverty – are also an essential point of contact for work with women which is about empowerment.

Without specific networks of these kinds, work with women and girls will exclude all too many perspectives, and feminist practice will again become a code word for White, middle-class practice. Women who work in positions and in forums where decisions are made, particularly about funding and resourcing, need to work in ways that are actively counter-cultural. Timetables for consultation need to be realistic; programmes for bids to be made need to be drawn up in ways which encourage all groups to participate, and notice needs to be taken of the groups which are absent from the decision-making process. Women's groups which find themselves in competition for funding need to find ways to collaborate, and potential conflicts between mainly White women's groups and Black groups need to be attended to very carefully.

Alliances can only be made to work if they are undertaken with the involvement and support of organisations. They cannot rely solely on the good relationships between individuals. Once these patterns of organisational coalitions are in place, then the long-term work of exploring the points of difference and the points of commonality can be undertaken. At present, this is often undertaken at the level of avowed principles, shared values and aims. There may exist shared commitments to, for example, anti-oppressive practice. Unfortunately, stating a set of principles is not usually the problem. It is at the point of perceived failure to act according to apparently shared principles that coalitions break down.

Tackling the ideological agenda of danger and safety

Reading the work of Maude Stanley again in the current climate and then referring to the archives of material from the girls' work movement of the 1970s and 1980s, it is hard not to conclude that work with girls and young women is closer in spirit and preoccupations to the agenda of the 1890s than it is to the exhilarating, libertarian agendas of the much more recent past.

Part of the impact of the current shifts in funding has been to re-focus the agenda of concern around issues of the protection of girls and young women. There has also been a renewed concern with motherhood as the place from which women's contribution to society is most frequently assessed. From the point of view of a feminist practice which challenges the subordination of women, this is a profoundly conservative agenda, which reinforces the sense of girls and young women as victims or as existing to nurture and to meet the needs of others. It infantilises young women and promotes a continuing state of dependency. It suggests a false unity among girls and young women: a unity which seems to derive from either the presence of threats and the need for protection, or, failing all else, a unity which derives from the capacity to bear children.

The commitment to self-activity and self-definition which characterised the early initiatives of the girls' work movement was not alone strong enough to prevent this agenda from re-emerging. It is also difficult to believe the protestations of youth workers that the use of such discourse in funding proposals is merely a convenience and that empowering practice continues, despite the framing of work by very conservative language. Methods which involve the assessment of project success in terms of the attainment of key outcomes and targets clearly mean that the language of funding bodies has its impact. It does not take long to establish itself in our own thinking.

Perhaps the persistence of these ideologies of risk and protection and of motherhood suggest the need for a very long-term feminist strategy, capable of persisting as a counter-discourse over generations, capable of becoming an alternative 'common sense' which can achieve the adherence of more than one generation of women.

As well as celebrating diversity and self-activity, it will continue to be necessary to offer alternative accounts of what it means to be a mother and of the nature of female sexuality. The discourse of women's rights and women's potential clearly has staying power. We also need to keep creating and sharing alternative imaginings in which independence and motherhood, pleasure and risk, sexuality and safety are not in opposition to one another.

Informal education with girls and young women could ally itself with feminist intellectual work again, including work which is taking place in women's studies. It must certainly ally itself with feminist work in the mass media, where much of the creation of meanings about femininity takes place. It must also value and connect with the work of film-makers, musicians, artists, novelists and poets who resource the imagination.

Working across generations: Who are the young women?

On several occasions when I have been discussing this book in the past year, older women workers who have been involved in work with girls and young women for perhaps fifteen years mentioned the need for new thinking about sustaining the work, sustaining themselves as workers and communicating the values and philosophy of feminist youth work practice to a new generation of young women. A number of strategies have been adopted, and there is clearly a commitment and recognition of the need for a variety of responses. The most commonly mentioned are the following.

• There is a perceived need for more women to take their concerns and commitments into senior management positions where the allocation of resources and the formulation of policies can be influenced in the interests of girls and young women. There has been a tendency for women who seek to occupy such senior positions to be seen as 'selling out'. Perhaps the tendencies which create them as 'token women in bureaucracies' or as 'honorary men' need to be addressed instead. An organisational strategy which is explicit about the relationships between feminists who occupy different roles and positions of power in organisations needs to be addressed. Networking among women managers is obviously important, but equally obviously, it is less important than networking between women managers and their subordinates.

• The role of staff development and training has been identified for a number of years as critical to the continuing strength of feminist work. Again, a number of strategies have been adopted, ranging from those which focus on enabling women workers, whether part-time or full-time, to develop their own understandings of their position as women, through to strategies to ensure the development of feminist competence through staff appraisal schemes! As long ago as 1984, the working group which produced the document *Starting from Strengths* (Bolger and Scott, 1984) commissioned an extension report on women, training and change which made the following observations in its conclusions:

> Women are not a homogeneous group whose needs can be met if only 'the one right formula' is found. What is important is that women can choose and that their right to choose is respected by those who are responsible for ensuring that women part-time and voluntary workers have the training and support they deserve.
> Some women do derive a tremendous amount of support and learning from meeting together in small, women-only groups, where work and personal feelings concerning work are discussed and shared. This will maintain the momentum for change within the roles and opportunities open to women and girls. (Lacey and Trent, 1984, p.8)

• Women identified the need for more explicitly-acknowledged mentor relationships which have the purpose of valuing work and of allowing expertise and understandings to be shared. Mentoring involves a one-to-one relationship in which there is an explicit commitment to the development of individuals within the workplace, and even within the career structure. It has been developed as an alternative to managerial supervision and has its roots in traditions of supervision and support which are based on non-hierarchical relationships. However, it also enables a recognition of the place of sponsorship within hierarchies and the need for those who are not part of the traditions of the '(White) men only culture' to find ways of counteracting the tendencies of White, male-dominated organisations simply to reproduce themselves. The practice of mentoring is becoming particularly important for Black professionals, and Black women have much to gain from such a process.

● Women identified the need for networking at all levels, and between women working at all levels in the system and with different levels of experience. Networking needs to occur purposefully and explicitly. It should not be merely a reproduction of social support networks, which may, by their very nature, be fairly homogeneous and exclusive. It is also important to clarify the kind of support women can expect from one another in workplace or professional settings. Just as the boundaries between friendship and work may need to be clarified with young women, so women workers need to be very explicit about what their expectations are of one another in relation to giving and receiving professional support. There is a demonstrable need for support systems for strong, experienced and competent women workers. All too often, professional support is offered only to those who are perceived to be weak or inexperienced or incompetent in some way.

Feminism across generations

It should be clear from the argument of this book (and many others) that the transition from being a girl to being a woman is not a natural one. It is socially marked by motherhood, by the acceptance of adult responsibilities for care of dependants and by negotiation of a relationship to heterosexuality. It may also be marked by a relation of economic and social independence from parents and by release from compulsory schooling.

This social and economic independence is not absolute. Dependence on parents and parent substitutes may well be exchanged for dependence on benefits or dependence on a male partner. All the negotiations which occur in this transition are potentially the subject matter of informal education; they form the contested landscape of femininities.

If women are to become a group asserting a political agenda in relation to rights, sexuality and motherhood, the form that the transition from girlhood to womanhood takes will be an essential part of that agenda. It is clear that such a political grouping, calling itself feminist, will be characterised by its positive commitment to diversity and the recognition and acknowledgement of difference.

Within feminist writings and discussions, the issue of negotiations about the meaning of the term 'feminism' across generations has paid some attention to the difficulties and potentials of the mother–daughter relationship as a political issue for feminism. It seems very important to me that feminist politics can be identified with the difficult and obstreperous daughters, if it comes to a fight between them and the controlling good-enough mothers. At the same time, feminist politics needs to be able to embrace the power of motherhood and offer alternative forms of adult womanhood, including motherhood, to young women.

Informal education with girls and young women in community settings has something to offer to this process of feminist politics, because its starting point is always future-orientated. It is about girls looking into the future (and changing the world on the way).

References

Aggleton, Peter, Rivers, Kim and Warwick, Ian (1990) *AVERT/AIDS: Working with Young People*, Horsham: AVERT.

Anthias, Floya and Davis, Nira Yuval (1991) *Racialised Boundaries: Race, nation, gender, colour and class in the antiracist struggle*, London: Routledge.

Arendt, Hannah (1986) 'Communicative Power' in Lukes, Stephen (ed.) *Power*, Oxford: Basil Blackwell.

Arnold, Julie, Askins, Dave, Davies, Randal, Evans, Steve, Rogers, Alan and Taylor, Ted (1981) *The Management of Detached Work: How and Why*, Leicester: NAYC Publications.

Ashby, Anna (1994) 'Asian young women act it out', *Youth Clubs*, April.

Baker, John (1987) *Arguing for Equality*, London: Verso.

Batsleer, Janet (1986) *Project Report*, Wakefield Youth Service.

Beetham, David (1991) *The Legitimation of Power*, London: Macmillan.

Beetham, Margaret (1996) *A Magazine of Her Own? Domesticity and Desire in the Woman's Magazine 1800–1914*, London: Routledge.

Bolger, Steve and Scott, Duncan (1984) *Starting from Strengths*, Leicester: National Youth Bureau.

Browne, Susan E., Connors, Debra and Stern, Nancy (1985) *With the Power of Each Breath: A Disabled Women's Anthology*, Pittsburgh: Cleis Press.

Bryan, Beverley, Dadzie, Stella and Scafe, Suzanne (1985) *The Heart of the Race*, London: Virago.

Burman, Erica (1994) *Deconstructing Developmental Psychology*, London: Routledge.

Burman, Erica (in press) 'False Memories, True Hopes and the Angelic: Revenge of the Postmodern on Therapy', *New Formations*.

Butler, Judith (1989) *Gender Trouble: Feminism and the subversion of identity*, New York: Routledge.

Butler, Sandra and Wintram, Claire (1991) *Feminist Groupwork*, London: Sage.

Campbell, Beatrix (1993) *Goliath: Britain's Dangerous Places*, London: Methuen.

Carpenter, Val and Young, Kerry (1986) *Coming in from the Margins: Youth Work with Girls and Young Women*, Leicester: National Association of Youth Clubs.

Chauhan, Vipin (1989) *Beyond Steel Bands n Somosas*, Leicester: National Youth Bureau.

Cockburn, Cynthia (1987) *Two-track Training: Sex Inequalities and the Y.T.S*, Basingstoke: Macmillan.

Cole, Pam (1989) 'Northern College, Barnsley and Wakefield Partnership', *Replan Bulletin*, No.3, Summer.

Connolly, Clara (1990) 'Splintered Sisterhood: Anti-Racism in a Young Women's Project', *Feminist Review*, No.36, Autumn.

Coward, Rosalind (1984) *Female Desire*, London: Paladin.

Davies, Bernard (1986) *Threatening Youth: Towards a national youth policy*, Milton Keynes: Open University Press.

Dennis, Jill (1982) 'How dare you assume I made a mistake? Young Black Women with Children', *Working with Girls Newsletter*, No.9, May/June.

Dennis, Norman (1993) *Rising Crime and the Dismembered Family*, London: Institute of Economic Affairs Health and Welfare Unit.

Dennis, Norman and Erdos, George (1993) *Families without Fatherhood* (Foreword by A.H. Halsey), London: Health and Welfare Unit.

DES, WO and NACYS (Department of Education and Science, Welsh Office and National Advisory Council for the Youth Service) (1989) *Youth Work with Girls and Young Women*, January, London: HMSO.

DfE (Department for Education) (1994) *Education Act 1993: Sex Education in Schools*, Circular no.5/94.

DHSS and WO (Department of Health and Social Security and Welsh Office) (1988) *Working Together: A guide to interagency co-operation for the protection of children from abuse*, London: HMSO.

DoH (Department of Health) (1992) *The Health of the Nation: A Strategy for Health in England*, Cm 1986, London: HMSO.

Dickinson, Sakinna (1995) personal correspondence with author.

Dominelli, Lena and McLeod, Eileen (1989) *Feminist Social Work*, Basingstoke: Macmillan.

Driver, Emily and Droisen, Audrey (1989) *Child Sexual Abuse: Feminist Perspectives*, Basingstoke: Macmillan.

Eastham, Derek (1990) 'Plan It or Suck It and See? A Personal View of the Canklow Community project' in Darvill, Giles and Smale, Gerald (eds) *Partners in Empowerment: Networks of Innovation in Social Work*, London: National Institute for Social Work.

Erault, Michael and Kelly, Dennis (1994) *Preparatory Study to Explore the Scope for Developing N.V.Q. Standards for Youth and Community Work*, Brighton: University of Sussex.

Erikson, Eric (1968) *Identity, Youth, and Crisis*, New York: Norton.

Foucault, Michel (1980) *Power/Knowledge: Selected interviews and other writings*, New York and London: Harvester Wheatsheaf.

Frazer, Elizabeth and Lacey, Nicola (1994) *The Politics of Community*, Hemel Hempstead: Harvester Wheatsheaf.

Freire, Paolo (1972) *The Pedagogy of the Oppressed*, London: Penguin.

Gilroy, Paul (1993) 'One Nation Under a Groove' in *Small Acts*, London: Serpent's Tail.

Green, Steph (1995) 'Sex and Drugs and RocknRoll', paper presented at North West Detached Workers Conference, unpublished.

Gregson, Nicky and Lowe, Michelle (1994) *Servicing the Middle Classes: Class, gender and waged domestic labour in Britain*, London: Routledge.

Griffin, Christine (1993) *Representations of Youth: The Study of Youth and Adolescence in Britain and America*, Cambridge: Polity.

Hansford, Lorraine (1993) 'Student Placement Report', Manchester Metropolitan University, unpublished.

Haraway, Donna (1991) 'Reading Buci Emecheta: Contests for Women's Experience in Women's Studies' in *Simians, Cyborgs and Women: The Re-invention of Nature*, London: Free Association Books.

Hemmings, Susan (ed.) (1982) *Girls are Powerful: Young Women's Writings from Spare Rib*, London: Sheba.

Herbert, Carrie (1992) *Sexual Harassment in Schools*, London: David Fulton.

Herman, Didi (1994) *Rights of Passage: Struggles for Lesbian and Gay Equality*, Toronto: University of Toronto Press.

Herrnstein, Richard and Murray, Charles (1994) *The Bell Curve: Intelligence and class structure in American life*, New York and London: Free Press.

Hetrick, E. and Martin, D. (1984) 'Egodystonic homosexuality: A developmental view', in Hetrick, E. and Stein, T. (eds) *Innovations in Psychotherapy with Homosexuals*, Washington DC: American Psychiatric Press.

Hill Collins, Patricia (1991) *Black Feminist Thought: Knowledge, Consciousness and the Politics of Empowerment*, New York: Routledge.

Holland, Janet, Ramazanoglu, Caroline, Sharpe, Sue and Thomson, Rachel (1994) 'Power and Desire: The Embodiment of Female Sexuality', *Feminist Review*, No.46, Spring.

Holman, Bob (1994/5) 'Urban Youth: Not an Underclass', *Youth and Policy*, No.47, Winter.

hooks, bell (1984) *Feminist Theory: From margin to center*, Boston, Mass: South End Press.

hooks, bell (1989) 'Feminism: A transformational politic' in *Talking Back: Thinking Feminist, Thinking Black*, London: Sheba.

hooks, bell (1992) 'Selling hot pussy' in *Black Looks: Race and representation*, London: Turnaround.

Hudson, Annie (in press) *Troublesome Girls?*, Basingstoke: Macmillan.

Hulme Girls' Project (1984) *Young Women with Children Report 1981–4*, Manchester: Hulme Girls' Project.

Humm, Maggie (1992) *Feminisms: A reader*, Hemel Hempstead: Harvester Wheatsheaf.

Hussain, Rehana (1994) *Student Placement Report*, Manchester Metropolitan University.

Hyatt, Susan B. with Caulkins, D. Douglas (1992) '*Putting bread on the table*', *The Women's Work of Community Activism*, Occasional Paper No.6, Bradford: Work and Gender Research Unit, University of Bradford.

Irigaray, Luce (1980) 'When Our Lips Speak Together', *Signs: Journal of Women in Culture and Society*, Vol.6, No.1.

Jamdagni, Laxmi (1980) *Hamari Rangili Zindagi: Our Colourful Lives, A report by Laxmi Jamdagni of her work with Asians Girls in the Midlands*, Leicester: NAYC Publications Special Report Series.

Jeffs, Tony and Smith, Mark K. (1994) 'Getting the job done: Training for youth work, past present and future', *Youth and Policy*, Spring.

Jones, Carol and Mahoney, Pat (1989) *Learning our Lines: Sexuality and Social Control in Education*, London: Women's Press.

Jordan, June (1989) 'Report from the Bahamas' in *Moving Towards Home: Political Essays*, London: Virago.

Kelly, Liz (1988) *Surviving Sexual Violence*, Cambridge: Polity.

Kinsey, Alfred (1948) *Sexual Behaviour in the Human Male*, Philadelphia: W.B. Saunders.

Kinsey, Alfred (1953) *Sexual Behaviour in the Human Female*, Philadelphia: W.B. Saunders.

Kutub, Yasmin (1995) 'Making Youth Work Accessible to Black Women in the North East of England', *Youth and Policy*, No.49, Summer.

Lacey, Fran and Sprent, Sue (1984) *Women, Training and Change Patterns for Development*, Extension Report No.4, Leicester: National Youth Bureau.

Lal, Sushma and Wilson, Amrit (1986) *But my cows aren't going to England: A study of how families are divided*, Manchester Law Centre.

Lees, Sue (1986) 'A New Approach to the Study of Girls', *Youth and Policy*, No.16.

Lorde, Audre (1984) 'Uses of the Erotic: The Erotic as Power', in *Sister Outsider*, Freedom, Calif: Crossing Press.

Lukes, Stephen (ed.) (1986) *Power*, Oxford: Basil Blackwell.

MacKinnon, Catharine (1982) 'Feminism, Marxism, Method and the State: An Agenda for Theory', in Keohane, N.O., Rosaldo, Michelle and Gelph, Barbara C. (eds) *Feminist Theory: A Critique of Ideology*, Brighton: Harvester Wheatsheaf.

Mama, Amina (1989) *The Hidden Struggle: Statutory and voluntary sector responses to violence against Black women in the home*, London: Race and Housing Research Unit.

Manchester Young Lesbian Group (1992) *The First Three Years*, Manchester: Shades City Centre Project.

McCabe, Tricia and McRobbie, Angela (1981) *Feminism for Girls: An Adventure Story*, London: Routledge and Kegan Paul.

McFadyean, Melanie (1986) 'Youth in Distress: Letters to Just Seventeen', *Health Education Journal*, Vol.45, No.1.

McIntosh, Mary (1993) 'Queer Theory and the War of the Sexes' in Bristow, Joseph and Wilson, Angelia (eds) *Activating Theory*, London: Lawrence and Wishart.

Mies, Maria and Shiva, Vandana (1993) *Ecofeminism*, London: Zed Books.

Milson, Fred (1970) *Youth Work in the 1970's*, London: Routledge and Kegan Paul.

Mitchell, Juliet and Rose, Jacqueline (eds) (1982) *Feminine Sexuality: Jaques Lacan and the ecole freudienne*, London: Macmillan.

Moore, Gail (1994) *Student Placement Report*, Manchester Metropolitan University.

Morris, Lydia (1994) *Dangerous Classes: The Underclass and Social Citizenship*, London: Routledge.

Murray, Charles (1994) *The Emerging British Underclass*, London: Institute of Economic Affairs Health and Welfare Unit.

Nava, Mica (1992) *Changing Cultures: Feminism, youth and consumerism*, London: Sage.

Newman, Eileen and Ingram, Gina (1989) *The Youth Work Curriculum*, London: Further Education Unit.

Nicholls, Cath (1994) conversation with the author.

NOWGYW (National Organisation for Work with Girls and Young Women) (no date) *Background and History*, London: Amazon Press.

Osborne, Liz and Walmsley, Michelle (1995) 'The National Organisation for Work with Girls and Young Women (1981–1994)', Manchester Girls' Project, unpublished.

Parmar, Pratibha (1989) 'Black Lesbians' in Phillips, Angela and Rakusen, Jill (eds) *The New Our Bodies, Ourselves*, Harmondsworth: Penguin.

Pearson, Geoffrey (1983) *Hooligan! A History of Respectable Fears*, Basingstoke: Macmillan.

Peerman, Poddy and Keenan, Julia (1993) *Hag Fold Young Women's Centre Aims and Objectives 1993*, Wigan Youth Service, internal document.

Phillips, Angela and Rakusen, Jill (eds) (1989) *The New Our Bodies, Ourselves*, Harmondsworth: Penguin.

Phoenix, Ann (1991) *Young Mothers?*, Cambridge: Polity.

Quinn, Sue (1993) 'Let's advocate', *Youth Clubs*, Vol.73, September.

Rich, Adrienne (1980) 'Compulsory Heterosexuality and Lesbian Existence' in *On Blood, Bread and Poetry*, London, Virago.

Ronan, Alison (1994) Dissertation Proposal, Manchester Metropolitan University.

Rossi, Hugh (1988) *Great Britain Local Government Acts 1987 and 1988 Annotated by Sir Hugh Rossi*, London: Shaw and Sons.

Sawbridge, Muriel and Spence, Jean (1991) *The dominance of the male agenda in community and youth work*, University of Durham.

Schneider, Margaret (1989) 'Sappho was a Right On Adolescent', *The Journal of Homosexuality*, Vol.17, Nos 1/2.

Seabrook, Jeremy (1978) *What went wrong? Working people and the ideals of the labour movement*, London: Gollancz.

Selman, Peter and Glendinning, Caroline (1994/5) 'Teenage Parenthood and Social Policy', *Youth and Policy*, No.47, Winter.

Sivanandan, A. (1990) 'Left, right and Burnage', in *Communities of Resistance: Writings on Black Struggles for Socialism*, London: Verso.

Smith, Mark (1988) *Developing Youth Work: Informal education, mutual aid and popular practice*, Milton Keynes: Open University Press.

Solomos, John (1993) *Race and Racism in Britain*, Basingstoke/London: Macmillan.

Stanley, Maude (1890) *Clubs for Working Girls*, London: Macmillan.

Szirom, Tricia and Dyson, Sue (1986) *Greater Expectations: A Source Book for Working with Girls and Young Women*, Learning Development Aids.

Taylor, Tony (1987) 'Youthworkers as Character-builders: Constructing a Socialist Alternative' in Jeffs, Tony and Smith, Mark (eds) *Youth Work*, Macmillan.

Terry, Izzy, Davis, Marilyn and O'Neill, Nola (1993) 'In the Neighbourhood', *Youth Clubs*, Vol.74, October.

Thompson, Dai (1985) 'Anger', in Browne, Susan E., Connors, Debra and Stern, Nancy (eds) *With the Power of Each Breath: A Disabled Women's Anthology*, Pittsburgh: Cleis Press.

Thomson, Rachel and Scott, Sara (1991) *Learning about Sex: Young women and the social construction of sexual identity*, London: Tufnell Press.

Trimbell, June (1990) *Equality of Opportunity Provision for Girls and Young Women in the Full-time Sector of the Northern Ireland Youth Service*, Belfast: Youth Action Northern Ireland, May.

Troiden, Richard R. (1989) 'The Formation of Homosexual Identities', *The Journal of Homosexuality*, Vol.17, Nos 1/2.

TUC (1995) *Civil Rights for Disabled People: A TUC statement*, London: TUC.

Ward, David and Mullender, Audrey (1992) 'Empowerment and Oppression: An Indissoluble Pairing for Contemporary Social Work', *Critical Social Policy*, No.32, Autumn.

Weller, Paul (1987) *Sanctuary: The Beginning of a Movement?*, London: Runnymede Trust.

Williams, Raymond (1989) 'The Idea of Community' in *Resources of Hope: Culture, democracy, socialism*, London: Verso.

Williamson, Judith (1986) *Consuming Passions: The dynamics of popular culture*, London: Boyars.

Wilson, Melba (ed.) (1994) *Healthy and Wise: The essential health handbook for Black women*, London: Virago.

Young, Iris Marion (1994) 'Gender as Seriality: Thinking about Women as a Social Collective', *Signs: Journal of Women in Culture and Society*, Vol.19, No.3.

Young, Kerry (1992) 'Work with Girls and Young Women: Losing the Purpose?', *Youth Clubs*, Vol.67, April.

Youth Support Project (1986) *Annual Report*, Manchester: Project Report.

Youth Work Unit (1983) *Looking Beyond Street Level: Detached Youth Work with Young Women*, Leicester: National Youth Bureau.

Zion Community Health and Resource Centre (1993–4) *Amidst the Change*, Manchester: Project Report.

Index

Confronting Prejudice

Lesbian and gay issues in social work education

Janette Logan, Sheila Kershaw, Kate Karban, Sue Mills,
Joy Trotter and Margo Sinclair

This book brings lesbian and gay issues to the centre of the debate on anti-oppressive practice. It is an accessible and practical guide to the subject for all involved in student learning, aiming to provide practice teachers and educators with tools to help students develop their understanding of the effects of heterosexism as well as providing strategies for positive practice.

Part 1 considers:

• the social background, raising important issues about the ways in which lesbians and gay men are marginalised in society and the subsequent reflection in social work education and practice • the legal framework within which social workers and probation officers operate, drawing attention to some of the tensions and dilemmas facing practitioners attempting to develop anti-discriminatory and anti-oppressive practice • a framework within which to develop non-homophobic and non-heterosexist practice within the Diploma in Social Work, raising important issues which need to be addressed both within the academic institutions and the practice learning environment • how to facilitate students' learning in relation to anti-discriminatory and anti-oppressive practice with lesbian and gay service users • the assessment of students' competence within the academic and practice curriculum • a model of good practice in working with lesbians and gay men, offering practical suggestions which can be incorporated into existing policies and procedures.

Part 2 provides practical teaching and training materials.

1996   136 pages
Hbk   1 85742 359 3   £35.00   Pbk   1 85742 360 7   £15.95
Price subject to change without notification

arena

Empowerment
for *Life* *Skills*

A trainers' resource

Gaye Heathcote, Mary Child and Martin Edwards

This trainers' resource book consists of ideas, activities and exercises to develop or enhance lifeskills in ways which promote maximum personal autonomy. It is aimed at trainees, predominantly in pre-vocational and vocational settings, but is also highly suitable for those in full-time and part-time education. The book has been successfully piloted not only with trainees in the UK and in Europe (mainstream and special needs), but also in the context of training-the-trainer courses. It is ideal for schools, youth services, FE colleges and youth training agencies wishing to stage their own in-house courses in lifeskills and personal and social education.

The book consists of four major sections: Assertiveness, Communication, Job Seeking and Lifeskills. The grouping of the activities enables the user to create courses based around specific skill areas or to combine the sections to cover more than one skill area. Activities can also be used on an *ad hoc* basis as stand-alone units and are set at different levels to suit different needs.

Gaye Heathcote is Head of the Department of Humanities and Applied Social Studies at Manchester Metropolitan University.

1996   240 pages   Ringbinder   1 85742 351 8   £49.50

Price subject to change without notification